MW01031612

The Old Car Nut Book #2

"Where More Old Car Nuts Tell Their Stories"

Created and Edited by David Dickinson

Evancourt Press
Seattle, Washington

ISBN 978-0-9898065-1-0

Published in the United States by Evancourt Press

Dedication

This second volume in The Old Car Nut Book series is dedicated to my son, Evan, who inspires me each and every day.

Excerpts from
The Old Car Nut Book
Volume 2

Before I knew it, the first leg of my road trip was finished, and it was time to get on the expressway for the last fifty miles. I eased into the gas and listened to the huge Holley carb suck air, the tailpipes bark that wonderful song, and watched the speedo climb to 60...70...80 before settling back to the speed limit (sorta) and thinking of that day that I made good on my promise.

Excerpt from Psychiatrist with a Black Convertible Top
by Tom Glide

News traveled fast. One weekend before the show, Rich got a call from Joe Bailon inviting him to his home for a BBQ. Joe said that he had heard about our get together and he and Gene Winfield wanted to talk to Rich about it.

Excerpt from The History of West Coast Kustoms and How
Paso Came About *by Penny Pichette*

The car spent the next 42 years in one barn or another until I retired in 2010. I rented a trailer and winched the car out of the barn it had spent the last dozen years in and hauled it home. I changed the oil in the engine, transmission, and rear end. Then, I bought a new battery, 4 spark plugs, and 5 gallons of gas. After I took the Tillotson carb apart and sprayed carb cleaner all over it, I put it back together with the same gaskets. It started up as if it had been running the previous week.

Excerpt from Model A in the Barn *by Dale Erickson*

We put the Lincoln dashboard in it and I lettered notes and lyrics on it. On the left side of the steering column, above the gauges, I put "Son, you're gonna drive me to drinkin' ..." and on the other side, just to the right of the clock, I finished with "if you don't stop drivin' that Hot Rod Lincoln". The chrome and stainless on the dash shined like new and the lettering really made it all pop. It got a nice new leather interior, not an old ragged ass seat that was in there and stuff like that. We did everything to make it a show car.

Excerpt from Hot Rod Lincoln *by Bob Davidson*

The materials and methods that make this car up are long ago forgotten and irreplaceable. Indeed, this car is a rarity. I took a whiff of that unmistakable aroma, a mixture of 70 year old mohair, rubber, oil, gasoline, and an exhaust that hasn't been emasculated by a catalytic converter and it took me back to my youth, when horsepower was king. This was a time when romance was found at the sock hop or the soda shop, not on a dating site, when teenagers were wrenching on old iron instead of playing video games.

Excerpt from Some Things Just Go Together
by Dave Darby

Not oblivious to the fact that what I was doing was against school policy, the law, and the most basic of common sense, I let off the gas and let the car roll to a parking space where I left it to smolder, so to speak. The smoke from the burnout lingered, wafting out of the wheels wells, incriminating the car in the nefarious event. I had gotten out and walked away, watching from a distance as the police arrived. They inspected it, made some notes, looked around ... and left. I guess they had bigger fish to fry than investigating a burnout where they couldn't prove who had done it.

Excerpt from Asphalt Eating Olds *by David Dickinson*

Now the big problem: how to join Greg's old engine and my Chev body in holy matrimony. It was time for me to reach deep into my bag of tricks and solve the problem. I had a secret weapon - a weapon that none of my non-mechanically challenged buddies could resist. I had at my disposal a weapon that was so powerful that it was second only to the allure of attention from pubescent females. I had pizza!

Excerpt from Pizza Sauce and 30W Oil *by Lance Lambert*

The light went to green and I smiled as Lois had failed to Power brake that heavy old Plymouth at all. About mid intersection, I grabbed second and just as I was going to slam the go button to the floor, I heard it just off to my left. WHOOSH ... the huge white whale went past me. The next three lights were repeats of the first, as Lois took me to the woodshed, stop light after stop light.

Excerpt from Commando Power *by Mike Godwin*

We just kept coasting, knowing it was all downhill to where the car should be. There was only one traffic light and two stop signs on the route. We made the green light in the most congested area and kept on coasting, and ran the stop sign at 19th Street and another one at 6th Ave., allowing us to roll into the parking lot at the depot. Across the street was a grocery store/gas station where we bought a few cents' worth of gas and when my dad came home from work, he drove the car the block and a half to our house.

Excerpt from Still In the Game *by Denny Hall*

One great thing about this car is that it was my wife's Daddy's car and money is almost no object. So, when it needs something it gets it. The one exception to that rule would be the exterior paint. While fairly nice looking, even from a short distance, it's not perfect and that's just fine. She's been in the family since new and like all of us, this grand old lady has earned her few dings and minor scratches and I consider them badges of honor or marks of courage, if you will. She is a survivor and I think she likes her new home.

Excerpt from Heroes, Promises, and Survivors
by Erich Bailey

Clearly, to those who were there, this was a very special re-uniting of a man and his dream. Charlie spent about two hours reminiscing about his prize '27 Packard. We took him on an abbreviated tour of the LeMay Collection at Marymount and then returned him to his home in Tacoma. That happened on a Thursday afternoon. The following Monday, I received a call from Charlie's wife. Her conversation was moving. She was thankful that Charlie had had an opportunity to visit his old friend, his '27 Packard. His wife then told me that Charlie had passed away over the weekend following his visit to LeMay.

Excerpt from Charley's Packard *by Clayton Stott*

With hands cupped to the glass and literally out of ourminds with excitement, we were describing to each other what we were seeing, though hardly paying attention to what the other was saying. While hanging on to boards and balancing on stacked trash, there came a voice from right behind us! "Would you like to see inside?"

Excerpt from Lucky *by Mike Vervalin*

Table of Contents

Acknowledgements

I can't say enough about all of the people that have rallied around The Old Car Nut Book series. From individuals that have submitted their stories, readers that have posted wonderful reviews on Amazon, journalists that have written reviews in magazines, radio talk show hosts that have invited me to share The Old Car Nut Book on air, and the many that have asked for this series to continue ... the support and positive comments have been overwhelming. The list of names is too long to list here and I don't want to leave anyone out. So, suffice it to say ... I know who you are and you know who you are. I will always be grateful.

"What really knocks me out is a book that, when you're all done reading it, you wish the author that wrote it was a terrific friend of yours and you could call him up on the phone whenever you felt like it. That doesn't happen much, though."

— J.D. Salinger, *The Catcher in the Rye*

If you see me as that person, please feel free to contact me whenever you feel like it. You can find my Email and phone number in the back of this book.

David Dickinson
Creator and Editor, The Old Car Nut Book series

Foreword

by Jeff Zurschmeide
Automotive journalist and author

I learned two things in High School - one is that I'm a writer, and the other is that I'm a car guy. I'm sure I learned some other stuff, too, mostly involving girls and rock music, but those are the two things that stand out.

I learned that I was a writer by joining the staff of my high school newspaper, where I met other writers and a journalism teacher by the name of Bob Litchfield. He taught us the basics of reporting the news - who, what, where, when, and how, and he taught us to put it all in 300 words with a cohesive structure. But that was all just mechanics. He really taught us that a good story is always about the people involved - the people who made things happen and lived through some events that changed them in some way.

I have never forgotten that lesson, because it speaks to the deepest part of the human experience. The stories that we tell each other about ourselves and about the events that shape who we are, teach us truths that do not change over generations or historical eras. In a sense, we tell the same stories over and over, with different casts of characters and different surroundings, because they are still true.

The stories in this book tell us about fathers and sons, brothers and sisters, families and friends as close as any family. They tell us about funny things that happened, sometimes poignant and sad things, and through all, inspiring stories of how we roll through life, beat the challenges in front of us, and get where we're going.

And then there are the cars, which never say a word but somehow manage to become characters in their own right. It's often said that cars are more than just a structure of metal, rubber, and whatever other bits might go into the machine. Old car nuts know this is true, but we don't often ask ourselves *why* this is true. Is it just that we imbue the machine with a personality created out of our own imaginations? I don't think so. If we as individuals projected the entire notion ourselves, then there would be no rhyme or theme to the stories that we hear – yet there is a remarkable similarity among cars of a given make and model.

I'm not a mystic trying to tell you that cars come with their own souls, but they do come with the structure and design and craftsmanship they were given by their creators, and that informs everything that comes after - whether a car is forgiving or evil-handling, prone to break down at the worst possible moment or somehow always managing to get you home before collapsing in the driveway. The character of a car is mostly born in the design studio and the factory.

Yet on top of that initial character, there is the individual history of each car through its working life. Every spilled cup of coffee, every pothole, every fender-bender, every botched repair or brilliant upgrade leaves a mark. Each car has a unique story, and that process transforms the machine from an identical creature of the assembly line to an individual. That's why people say that new cars lack soul – they simply haven't had time to mature yet. Cars grow up and grow old the same way we do.

We come to know our personal cars in their individuality. "No one can steal my car because no one but me knows how to work my solenoid," said my sister's boyfriend once upon a time, and he was likely correct. We understand every quirk and we know every trick when it comes to our own rides, because we have taken the time to get to know the car as an individual.

When you combine your intimate knowledge of your particular automobile with the timeless ideals that cars represent to us - freedom, power, beauty, and individuality - the resulting brew is pure magic. For generations, our cars have created the scenes in which we live our lives. They have transported us both physically and emotionally - and for some of us they have become our life's work.

This book is a set of stories about what happens when people meet cars, and what happens to both of them after. The cars bring their individuality to the party, but at the root the stories are about what we wanted, what actually happened, how we responded, and what we learned. That is our common ground and shared experience, and why we recognize each other and ourselves so clearly in these stories.

David Dickinson has done admirable work in collecting people's memories and putting them together to allow us to hear more of these familiar tales. The first volume simply let us all know that there was a place for our stories, and now the floodgates have opened. There are enough stories out there to fill dozens of volumes, so enjoy this collection today. Tomorrow's stories are already on the way.

Introduction

by David Dickinson

Book One in The Old Car Nut Book series has been well received in the marketplace and there are a lot more stories that old car nuts want to tell. As a result, Evancourt Press brings you the second installment in the series. This book is a continuation of the first book in the sense that the stories are personal in nature and told by people from all across America. There is not a particular focus, so the topics and events described vary in many ways.

In this volume you will find recollections of cars that have been stored for many years by dedicated owners and finally brought into the sunlight again, heartwarming accounts of old car guys serving other's needs, and some inside info on legendary cars and people. The Queen of Kustoms tells about the beginning of West Coast Kustoms. NW pinstriper and automotive icon, Bob Davidson, tells the story of the real car that inspired the song "Hot Rod Lincoln" and Tim Strange of Strange Motion and TV's Search and Restore shares an inspiring story of a customer that touched him and all that he came in contact with.

Not many people own a car for 50 or 60 years, but a handful of the guys that have tell their stories here. Can you imagine finding and buying back a '32 Ford that you owned as a teen ... after regretting selling it 50 years ago? Read the story here.

Some of the people in these pages tell their stories from the perspective of their younger selves, stepping back in time for the moment to tell it like it was. Others tell what it was like to work together with family members or best friends to create one of a kind cars or share exciting adventures.

The people are different in each story, but in the pages of this collection, we find just how similar events, fads, trends, and cars were across time and just how much the people around them have in common from one coast to another. There are not many aspects of our old car hobby that are left untold here.

As you thumb through the pages of this book, you have a private session with old car guys telling you just what is bantered about in a group of friends hanging out at their favorite car show or the never revealed details of events passed that you won't discover anywhere else.

If you enjoyed the first book in the series, you are going to love this book. It's full of stories of the famous and not so famous cars and people that make this hobby of playing in the old steel, glass, and rubber what it is. Passion runs deep on these pages and once again, you will laugh or cry, finding amazing revelations or relating to each event told. In all cases, you will be transported to the past and share in the experiences of people you can always relate with.

As you read, you will find time stand still for a moment, transporting you back to simpler times and more carefree people. You are about to enter the very private world of people you have never met, sharing stories that they have been longing to tell for many years. So, turn the page and get started. Delve into a whole new adventure with each story told and get lost in your mind's eye while you take a respite from the hectic regimen of everyday life. See you on the inside!

The Old Car Nut Book
Volume 2

Psychiatrist with a Black Convertible Top

by Tom Glide

I slid behind the wheel of the shiny red '67 Plymouth Belvedere convertible and prepared for a two-hour road trip to Detroit. With a twist of the Pentastar key, I heard that distinctive Chrysler starter noise and a well built 440 shriek to life and settle into a loud rhythmic rumble.

A non-car guy once described the sound that this car makes as a bunch of monkeys beating on the inside of a huge steel drum with baseball bats, but it's music to my ears.

The original 385 horses that this engine produced wasn't enough for a prior owner. Speed parts abound in it, making enough power to spin the wheels at 55 mph with a quick blip of the throttle.

I'd love to say it is mine, but the trip I'm embarking on is to return it to its rightful owner…my sixty something sister, Kathy. How she came to own it isn't the modern day Little Old Lady from Pasadena story that it appears to be.

I ratcheted the gated B&M shifter into drive and proceeded onto the highway, listening to the tires chirp with every shift from the Torqueflight transmission, feeling the breeze flow through the open car. The past few weeks had been rather hellish for me and I really needed a road trip in an old car on a sunny day to rewind myself. As I drove along the lakeshore, I remembered the phone call that came from my sister a few years ago.

"It's Dave, Tom…," she told me, "He has cancer."

I was shocked. Dave was one of my favorites. "The last time I'd seen him he was fine. How could this be? Where does he have it? What is his prognosis?"

"They gave him six months." was her reply.

The rest of that call was a blur. I listened to her tell me what the doctors found. I talked to Dave, not knowing what to say. I'm sorry? That just doesn't seem fair. I remembered telling both of them if there was anything I could do, just ask, and I'm there. It was really all I could do, but it still left me feeling helpless.

I rumbled past a small cement block building along the highway that was painted a god-awful purple color. The windows were covered with aging plywood and tall weeds were slowly consuming the property, but I remembered it as the pristine white store with a well-manicured yard that once stood there. Back in the day there was a small pond behind the store, stocked with hungry trout, which for a fee, the owner would let you fish. Dave used to take me there in his cool bright red '68 Plymouth Satellite convertible when he was dating my sister. On one trip back home, he floored it on the open highway. I could remember the sound of the four barrel carb sucking air into the 440 big block it had and sitting in the back seat watching the speedometer climb to 60…70…80 and beyond.

It all took my mind back to the day I got a second call from my sister, asking me to make good on my "anything I can do" promise.

On her way to work, a necessary evil when her mind was on Dave, she spotted the Belvedere that I'm driving today sitting dusty and forlorn at the side of the road with a for sale sign taped to the window. It took her back to a happier time, so she bought it with hopes it would do the same for Dave.

It was in decent shape and had a fresh 440, but it also had a quickie Earl Shieb paint job, and a lot of small details that needed repaired to make it drivable. The charging system didn't work, the front end alignment had serious negative camber, and it was toed out like a duck. A lot of lights did not work, but it did brighten Dave's spirits. She asked me to make it right so he could enjoy it. I couldn't have been happier to oblige her request.

Before I knew it, the first leg of my road trip was finished and it was time to get on the expressway for the last fifty miles. I eased into the gas and listened to the huge Holley carb suck air, the tailpipes bark that wonderful song, and watched the speedo climb to 60…70…80 before settling back to the speed limit (sorta) and thinking of that day that I made good on my promise.

Dave had to sit in a lawn chair and watch my son and I trace and repair the wiring problems, give it a spirit level and tape measure alignment, and shore up most of the issues. When we were satisfied it was useable, we cruised it to Eddie's Drive In and enjoyed burgers and shakes much like he and Kathy did back in the day.

Although he didn't get to drive it much, it was the perfect thing for his outlook on life. Even if they just went out to the garage and looked at it, friends and family were able to talk about happy times and better days when they visited, rather than sit and wonder what the hell to say.

A few months later, Dave passed away and the car sat entombed in Kathy's garage for two years. She couldn't even open the door and look at it. That was until I got a call from her a few weeks ago, asking if I could come and get it and get everything fixed properly. The Clinton Township Cruise on Gratiot Avenue was coming up and she'd like to take it out.

It was now running great and everything was working correctly as I sped down I-94 toward the city. More and more, I started seeing other classic and muscle cars heading in the same direction. It was perfect weather for the event. As I left the expressway and drove towards my sister's home, I was seeing throngs of cars already cruising the famed road even though the cruise didn't officially start for a few hours. The trip refreshed me and the hellish weeks that had weighed me down weren't even a memory when I pulled into my sister's driveway. I was looking forward to the cruise, too, and seeing all the cars.

A blast of the Dixie horn I installed as a surprise for her mentally handicapped son Jeff (who is a huge Dukes of Hazzard fan) brought Kathy to the door. She stood on her front porch smiling at the now cleaned up and repaired car. Her eyes welled up.

"Are there a lot of cars out already?" she asked.

"Yup…they are everywhere." I held out the keys. "Enjoy."

"Gosh it really looks and sounds great, Tom. But I have to get stuff ready for our barbeque later…" I noticed her shuffling about, avoiding looking at the car. "Why don't you take it for a lap and take Jeff." She handed the keys back to me.

Jeff and I did take a lap around the six-block section of Gratiot and were enjoying ourselves while we admired the vast array of really nice cars.

"This is cool!" he yelled as a dark brown Dodge Dart, reverberating that same big block rumble, pulled up next to us at a light. "But, I wish my dad was here."

He is Jeff … right here," I said tapping on his chest near his heart.

Although we were having fun, I couldn't help but feel this was something Kathy needed to do, so when the lap was done, I turned back toward her home. When we returned, Jeff was excitedly telling her all about the ride and how much fun it was.

I held out the keys again. "I do need to run to the store and it is at the end of the driveway. Maybe I should take it. You wanna come along Jeff?" she asked.

I watched as the two of them got in the car and pulled away. A right turn at the end of the block would take her straight to the grocery store and a left would take her to Gratiot and the cruise.

After a long pause, her left turn signal came on. I smiled. The doctor was in.

I hoped the ride led to a happier time and much needed healing.

Dwarf Car Nut

by Ernie Adams

Growing up in Harvard, Nebraska, almost everything my family used around the house came from the city dump which was, conveniently, right down the street. We would haul off anything that could possibly be used. From linoleum, aluminum, and zinc to electric motors, rags, and other items that most people considered un- usable, it was all consid- ered fair game to my family. If we couldn't use it, we'd sell it. There was even an old boy that would come by and pay a penny per pound for the old rags that we would drag home.

So, salvaging and saving odd items is a way of life for me. That's what I build things out of and I learned my trade from that old dump back home. As my kids were growing up, and when it was time for them to have a new bike, I would take them to the dump and we would find all of the old bicycle frames, handlebars, seats, sprockets, chains, and wheels we could and take them home. I'd point to the pile of parts and tell the kids "There's your new bike. Let me know how I can help you."

I built my first bike with a 5/8hp Briggs & Stratton motor and a dual exhaust system when I was 11 years old.

After dropping motors into tricycles and various wagons, I graduated to slightly larger projects. I've always loved to build and it always came easy. Many times when I've needed a tool, I made one. On all of the cars that I build, I fabricate panels, doors, dashboards, trim, bumpers, and grills out of scrap metal, often using tools that I have designed and built.

Like many old car nuts, my fascination with cars began in grade school where I would admire the cars of the time, draw them in school, and even use them in homework assignments when I could. I built a wooden car, sporting peanut butter jar lid headlights, that I could steer and my mother would pull me around town. As an early teen, I built a four passenger peddle car using bicycle wheels and metal bead rails with a body. Later, I built my first metal car using nine old refrigerators.

In my later teen years I tried hotrods, but just like out of an old Henry Gregor Felson novel, and after a couple of years with no driver's license, I learned the difference between hot-rodding and cruising. When you are cruising you don't need bucket seats and a 4 speed transmission. You only need a bench seat so your lady friend can sit close to you. It's much safer to show your car on the street than to show how fast it will go. As I grew older, I began to realize the beauty of the early American automobile.

I think old cars are meant to be driven and enjoyed on the road. I'm the guy that likes to see an old car with an updated drive train, dual exhaust, fender skirts, white wall tires of a normal size, and a decent low dollar paint job. I'd be happiest if I could go cruising at least once a week.

Many people know me these days as the Dwarf Car

King, Mr. Dwarf Car, Father of the Dwarf Car, and other variations because of the cars that I build from scratch, using the old materials I have made a habit of collecting my whole life. My first dwarf car was modeled after a '28 Chevy two-door sedan. This small replica was completed in 1965 and is the product of simple imagination and inge-nuity. I used an 18hp Wisconsin motor and built the car pretty much using a homemade hacksaw made from a chair frame, a hammer, and a chisel. I began construction having no real clear plan... just a vision in my mind. I didn't have a torch to shape the steel with so I learned to fold ¼ inch along the edges of all the body panels and fused it all with an arc welder. I used the steel from nine old refrigerators that I cut up in pieces. I didn't know how to form compound bends and so, I used all the natural bends of the early refrigerators.

This was the first Dwarf Car ever built and is now lovingly referred to as "GRANDPA DWARF." My original idea for it was to be a touring car with solid rubber tires. Later, I added a top, twelve inch pneumatic tires, and a two cylinder 13hp Onan motor. The car has features like a cloth interior with bucket seats, operational windows, and a vinyl top. Grandpa Dwarf is 9 feet long, 53 inches high and has a 73 inch wheelbase. It's pretty light at only 900 pounds. To this day, the '28 Chevy dwarf car is kept in running order and is still driven.

The term dwarf car actually emerged around 1979 or 1980 when Darren Schmaltz and I built the first two miniature racecars. We had attended motorcycle side hack races in Phoenix, Arizona and on the way home I commented on how the three wheeled racers were too slow in the corners. Darren chimed in that they could improve considerably by adding another wheel to help through the corners. I figured that adding a body would gain spectator appeal. Next thing you know, we were talking about building some cars and the brain storming started.

Daren told me, "If you build one, I'll build one." Before you could put spark to a torch, we were pulling parts out from the backyard and the Dwarf Car phenomenon began. I settled on a '34 Ford coupe design because they were so popular and Daren decided to build a '33 Dodge coupe body style. Both cars were built with a 73" wheelbase and 46" height. The little cars had all steel construction and were powered by motorcycle engines. I had a 350cc Honda engine in my backyard that I used for my '34 Ford Dwarf. Daren was able to find a Kawasaki  350cc 3 cylinder 2 stroke engine for his '33 Dodge Dwarf. The '34 Ford Dwarf Car was ready for a trial road test within a month, but Daren's '33 Dodge Dwarf was only halfway complete, but finished not long after.

We didn't have solid plans for racing these cars. We were just having fun playing in the old iron. But, people had seen the cars hauled around Phoenix and would stop to express their interest. Common questions were, what is this, where do they race, and where can I get one?

The first time the two Dwarf Racers finally hit the track was March 1981. Daren and I were able to run a few exhibition hot laps around a 1/8 mile dirt go cart track by the name of Arrowhead Speedway in Phoenix, Arizona. The cars were an instant attraction. As this new form of racing continued to grow, there had to be some regulation and one of the things that was required was that a dwarf racer be between a 1928 in 1948 model with all steel construction.

By September 1983, the Yavapai County Fair had a Demolition Derby and Dwarf Car races and it all took off from there. There were eleven drivers and each one knew this would be the beginning of something huge. Originally, each driver of a Dwarf Race Car selected a cartoon character to carry on their car as a mascot and fans of all ages could relate to their favorite car with the cartoon character.

My '42 Ford Dwarf Car was used as the official pace car for the last Dwarf Car race event ever held at Manzanita Speedway in Phoenix, Arizona. Manzanita Speedway opened in 1951 and closed their doors April 11, 2009 after 58 years of racing. Forty five Dwarfs registered for those last Dwarf Car races. My '42 Ford Dwarf Cruiser was driven by Daren Schmaltz, co-founder of the Dwarf Race Cars and his passenger was John Cain of the Dwarf Car Company.

The early Legend Race Cars were simply a name change from Dwarf to Legend and fenders added to a Dwarf Race Car built off of my jigs. Later in 1992, President and General Manager of Lowe's Motor Speedway, "Humpy" Wheeler and Elliot Forbes-Robinson, designed the fiberglass version for the Legend Cars. To this day Legend Cars use the Dwarf Car specifications with a 73 inch wheelbase, 60 inch width and 46 inch height.

I have an idea for a second generation of Dwarf Race Cars. I think the current body styles could be changed to those from 1949 through 1964. The wheel base would also change from 73" to 80" and the wheels could extend slightly outside the body if needed. I don't have the time or energy these days to head up this next generation, but I sure would like to see someone pick this up and run with it.

I had learned a lot about bending and shaping metal and wanted to expand my skills and put myself and my ideas to the test. Wanting to go beyond building the tough, yet simple race cars, I made plans to build a fully dressed Dwarf Car with fenders, chrome, and interior. This would be a street legal driver in the dwarf car dimensions. Remembering a '39 Chevy Saturday night cruise from my hometown, I set my sights on recreating a car in that image. I started with photos of a full size car and took all of my measurements from those photos, so everything would be to scale. It's not how a factory designer would go about things, but it worked for me.

I tracked down an old Toyota in an alley that had the twelve inch wheels I wanted and got the whole thing for free. By just using the whole Toyota drive train, everything was compatible. It took me 2½ years to complete the '39 and at nearly 1800 pounds, it is fully equipped with everything the real car had in it and is a solid car that easily cruises at highway  speeds. I've driven it over 54,000 miles in the 16 years I've had it on the road. I have a full-sized '39 Chevy twin to the '39 Chevy Dwarf. People love to see the two side by side where they can compare the authenticity of the '39 Chevy Dwarf when paired up with the full-sized '39 Chevy.

I enjoyed the car and the build process so much that I decided to build another. I fell in love with a '42 Ford convertible after seeing the movie "April Love," in 1957. I was especially fond of the convertible feature and the front grill of the '42 Ford compared to the '46, '47 and '48 model. After thinking long and hard, I made a decision to build a Dwarf '42 Ford Deluxe Convertible. I even fabricated a hydraulic convertible top that is fully operational. This is the car that was used as the official pace car for the last Dwarf Car race event ever held at Manzanita Speedway. In 2003, I drove this car from Maricopa, AZ to Wauconda, Illinois near Chicago, to meet the Mid-Americruise. I did the cruise from Waucondo, Illinois to Lincoln, Nebraska. The cruise made stops at several rod shops along the way and received the "Editor's Choice Award," from Rod and Custom Magazine.

I kept adding to my stable of Dwarf Cars with a '29 Ford "Hillbilly" car. It took me only three months to build this car that was inspired by a man I once met in Iowa. It is unique to say the least.

Never satisfied, I kept building. The next car is the well-known "Rebel Rouser" '49 Mercury. The '49s have always

been one of my favorite designs and this car is done in a very traditional style having been "Nose-and-Decked" and sits low with baby moon hubcaps and beauty rings, fender skirts, two spotlights, a Fulton-style sun visor, and Lakes pipes.

I followed up the '49 Mercury with a '34 Ford 2 door sedan replica finished in a survivor type of look. The chrome shines bright, but I wanted the body to look as it had been locked away for decades and so it sports a heavy patina and hand crafted, rusty spoke wheels with the Ford V8 hubcaps.

Several years ago, my son asked me what I thought should be done with all of my cars once I am gone. I said "Just sell them. I'll be done with them." While that was one way to look at it, it wasn't a very good idea in his mind. He told me he could never break them up and send them in different directions. He felt the collection should stay together. As a result, we set about putting together a museum where they could be displayed and enjoyed by people that stopped by to visit. Well, that proved to be a pretty good idea. People started asking for memorabilia; something they could take with them to remember and share the experience. So, we started making videos and tee shirts and opened a gift shop. We even have trading cards and window stickers. As part of the museum experience, we show videos and most of the time I sit with the small audience and watch along. To be honest, I enjoy every moment and really get a kick out of the reactions of the people as they watch.

I've carved a unique spot in the world and have enjoyed learning and creating at every step. Life is good around the old piles of metal and the creations that everyone seems to enjoy. Stop by and say hi sometime. I'll try to be here to welcome you personally. If we meet and you ask me which of my dwarf car creations is the best one, I'll reply with a simple "The best is yet to come!"

Member of the Family

by Rick Melvin

Our 1955 Chevrolet 210 Delray has a rich history and has been in the family since it first drove away from Gene Teague Chevrolet of Stayton, Oregon on January 18, 1955 by my Grandfather, Joseph Melvin. The original purchase price was $2670.05.

We have all heard stories of classic cars with low miles, in nearly new condition, and often wonder how such time capsules can exist in this world of go here, go there, do this today, and do that tomorrow. It seems that almost everyone these days has something planned and places to go that involve jumping in the car. The story of this time capsule of automotive history is simple, sad, and inspiring.

My grandparents drove the car basically to-and-from the grocery store every other week, a distance of approximately four miles round trip for many years. Garaged its entire life, the car remained in Salem, Oregon until 1982, when my Grandfather passed away. He had continued to drive the car regularly until his passing at 97 years old and the actual mileage on the vehicle at that time was 32,054.

The vehicle was then passed on to my Aunt and Uncle, John and Margi Melvin, of Tacoma, Washington. My uncle drove the car, but not much as the mileage shows. Having been a POW, he enjoyed driving the Chevy in parades in the Tacoma, Washington area that recognized military veterans. He was very proud of his service.

John and Margi had two children, Doug and Peggy. Grandpa's car had been promised to them when the proper time came. Tragedy however, would change those long range plans. Doug, a Vietnam helicopter pilot, was killed in a helicopter accident at the young age of 27. He was working for a logging company in Idaho at the time of his death. Peggy would later pass away from complications of cancer at age 54.

I think the reason the car hadn't already gone to either of them was because my uncle was still enjoying it and wasn't ready to pass it on quite yet. He really loved the car and liked to take all his old buddies into the garage, smoke their cigars, and reminisce about the "good ol' days."

Having always been close to both my aunt and uncle, I received a call one evening in 2004 from my Uncle John. He again stated that the plans for the car had been to pass it down to his children, which now was no longer possible, and asked me if I would like to have my grandfather's Chevrolet.

Honored to have been thought of that highly, I of course said I would love to have the car. He informed me that he wasn't quite ready to let me have it just yet and that he needed to drive the 100 miles or so to our house and make sure that I had adequate garage facilities to properly house his prized possession. A short time later, my aunt and uncle did come to visit and my garage arrangement met my uncle's demands.

Time passed and approximately three years later, a conversation with my uncle led to his wanting to sign the car over to me. He was now 86 years old and was concerned that he may not be able to renew his driver's license due to vision issues. So, on November 25, 2007, Uncle John drove the 1955 Chevrolet for the last time. He drove from Tacoma to Port Angeles and delivered the car to my place of business.

When we got the car home, my uncle shared with me all of the original documentation which came with the car. The original bill of sale signed by my grandfather; the original insurance contract; original license plates; original owner's service policy; and all original maintenance records. He then signed the title over to me.

Suddenly, we were both overcome with the enormity of the moment. A highly decorated WWII POW and Purple

Heart recipient, my uncle seldom showed emotion. What he was doing was passing down a significant part of his past. It was his father's pride and joy and his, as well. For me, it was now my responsibility to be "caretaker" of this icon of our family and, in time, to pass it on to my only son. Doing so was a promise I made to my uncle, to my family, and to myself.

After Uncle John and Aunt Margi left, I sat and looked at the Chevy, sitting in its newly dedicated parking space and shining like new. After a short while, I climbed into the passenger's seat and looked around the interior, reveling in the like new condition of the upholstery and carpeting. I rubbed my hand along the lower seat and felt the plastic wrap that the factory put around the seat side shell vinyl to protect it while in transit to its destined dealership, still intact and doing its job after more than 50 years. I can only imagine why it was never removed, but I am thankful that it is still there and one more thing that adds to the uniqueness of grandpa's car.

I opened the glove box and there, to my amazement, was my grandfathers' old and tattered wallet with his Oregon driver's license showing his birthdate as 1885. Behind the wallet, his driving glasses and the favorite old pipe that I remembered with its sweet fragrance were also waiting there for me to find. Surprised and excited, I called to question my uncle about my discovery. His response was that he had no idea what I was talking about. The reality was that he had planted these items for me to find. It was his one last gesture, adding to the overall heritage and significance of the car and our family history. That was just like my uncle … full of surprises.

Regrettably, my Uncle John passed away six months later. I'm at peace, knowing that he was able to give me something which meant so much to him while he was alive. Of course, the car will never be for sale, but forever be a part of our family.

Other than being a one family owned car with ridiculously low miles, our Chevy has a lot of other things that make it unique. Obvious to many old car guys, and even the casual observers at the car shows I sometimes venture out to with the '55, are the 265cid V-8 and Cast-Iron Powerglide automatic transmission, original factory Glacier Blue paint, stainless window vent shades, bumper guard extensions, factory chrome tissue dispenser, original spare

 tire with air, AND that original plastic on the lower part of the front seat.

The trunk even has the factory optional tool kit, which consists of a small ball peen hammer, pliers, three open end wrenches, and a spark plug socket. Everything is in original, unrestored condition with the tires, battery, and exhaust being the only replaced items. As of this date, actual mileage on the car is 38,842.

Both my grandfather & uncle performed their own maintenance. This included engine oil and filter changes, tire rotation, lubrication of chassis, and transmission services. In fact, my grandfather recorded regular oil changes on the back of an envelope, which I still have.

When I do take my pride and joy out and about, it is one of those cars that people gather around, impressed with its condition and amazed that it could look so good without having been restored. They ask a million questions about the car and its history. For me, those onslaughts of questions and people circling the car, looking in and around and up and down, are not an imposition at all, but rather a validation of my family's dedication to this old piece of iron, glass, paint, and rubber. They seem to see it the same as I do; an exceptional example of our automotive heritage and as one of those cars to cherish and preserve, not only for my family, but for the world of old car lovers to enjoy.

So, having made the promise to love, honor, and cherish this fine old lady, and to pass her down the line to my son, I can assure you that it will be a while until a fourth generation is tasked with the responsibility of this older member of the family. For now, I take great pleasure in my duties.

Mouse and Cat

by David Dickinson

In 1967, I was one of the proud teenage recipients of that cool little piece of paper called a driver's license. It was one of the first official pieces of ID a young person gets and I cherished it and the freedom it was going to provide.

We have all made mistakes and I made a huge mistake one night before the ink on my new license was even dry. That night was one I will never forget and although it started out innocently, it went bad from the start.

I had borrowed my folk's car and headed out to the local cruise spot where I ran into a couple of sisters I knew from a church youth group I belonged to. They always seemed innocent in their own way, but as I found out all too quickly that night had a wild streak, as well. When I ran into them, they asked me to join them in their car. Of course, being a red blooded American teen, I parked my car and  went over to theirs. Here's where the night started going south, so to speak.

"You drive!" one of the sisters said. Still enamored with my new license and thrilled to get behind the wheel of any car, I jumped into the driver's seat of their 1962 Corvair four door sedan. It was their parent's car and one that they shared between them. It wasn't the sportiest ride, but I was driving two girls around, so who was I to complain.

We joked and laughed as we cruised, comparing stories about our different high schools across town from each other. They thought they had a better basketball team and I was certain we had a better football team.

As we turned a corner to head back down the Ave, one of the sisters saw a guy from their school that she knew and started madly waving out the window at him. I could care less about the guy, but thought his '56 Ford was pretty cool. It was solid black; a shiny beast that would have caught my  eye on any day. Slightly raised in the rear and lowered in the front, it had a rake on it that any young driver would be proud of. Custom wheels reflected the street lights, giving off a yellow glow as we gave way for a red light.

He accelerated off the line at the first stop light the moment it changed. The sisters became anxious; each yelling for me to give chase as if they were Priscilla in pursuit of Elvis. I got caught up in the moment and sped up. The guy would not be engaged and he sped up even more. This went on for several blocks and a couple of turns. By the time we hit the intersection near the community college, we were doing 60 in a 35. Sitting in the parking lot of the mini mart on the corner of the intersection were two city police cars and suddenly one chase was over and another beginning. The two cop cars descended on us in flashes of red and I pulled over at the earliest possible moment.

The girls were immediately quiet, the boy in the black car no longer of any importance. One set of cops came to me and the other to the black Ford sitting 100 feet ahead. I knew I was in big trouble. This was not something I would have done normally.

The issuing of tickets became a blur. The police saw it for what it was; not a race, but a futile chase; more mouse and cat than cat and mouse. I drove myself back to my car and said my good-nights to the sisters and went home. The next three weeks before traffic court ground on me. I hated not having the whole thing over. I told my mother, but not my step dad. He never said anything and I don't know if she told him what had happened before it was all over. Of course, he eventually did find out.

When the day to go to court finally came, I had to go with my mom because I was a juvenile. As we sat on the bench toward the back of the court, waiting my turn, I searched for the other guy, but didn't really know him and wasn't really sure what he looked like. I did know his name. I don't remember it now, but I do remember when the deputy of the court called his name and he went before the judge.

The judge, a mid-fifties guy with short cropped grey-ing hair, looked over the file and then to the other kid and started reading him the riot act about going 60 in a 35 and how that kind of behavior would "not be tolerated in our city from our young drivers" with a few other choice words thrown in. In the end, he let the kid off with a warning and told him he'd better not ever show his face in court under these types of charges again. The kid walked past me, his back away from the judge and a slight smirk on his face, knowing he'd gotten off easy.

Before I could even reflect on what my fate might be, I heard my name. I stood and went before the judge. He looked at my file and then looked at me. He looked at the file again and looked back at me. With his eyes narrowed and a twist to his cheek he asked, rhetorically, "Didn't I just see all of the same info on that last young man's ticket?" He lifted the file from the stack of cases he had already passed judgment on. Momentarily scanning that file, he asked "Were you racing this other young man, Mr. Dickinson?"

He didn't give me time to respond before he told me that he was going to make an example of me and went on to tell me that my license, that ticket to freedom and passport to adventure that I so highly prized, was to be suspended for a period of six months. He closed by expressing his hope that I would learn my lesson and adjust my driving habits in the future. Then, he dismissed me with instructions to hand my license over to the court clerk, so much as to say … NEXT!

I spent the following six months taking the city bus to school or begging rides from friends and having to delay the purchase of my own first car. It wasn't a happy time, but it was a learning experience. From then on, I vowed to stay out of Corvairs with overly excitable sisters.

The History of West Coast Kustoms and How Paso Came About

by Penny Pichette

My husband, Rich, and I owned a burger place in the town of Sunnymead, California called "The Jet Drive-In" that was built in 1955. It got its name, I guess, because of the Air Force Base that was located there. Rich talked me into letting him buy a 1941 Chevy Pickup. It was an ugly, stock pea green truck. I was definite-

ly not thrilled, but he convinced me that we could use it for advertising for the drive-in, so I conceded.

He and a few other car guys would hang out together. One guy had a chopped Merc, another a 1956 Ford and the list goes on. All the cars were mild to wild customs with the exception of Rich's truck. He had painted it black with flames, shaved, lowered and whatever. He wanted to have it chopped but I said NO, NO, NO, but I was taking a plane trip to Connecticut and the plane was no sooner in the air than he took it to his friend Bob's yard and together, they chopped it. The next day he called to inform me what he had done. Oh well, too late now.

We had been going to Anaheim to a cruise night at Angelo's and thought it would be nice for the cars in Southern California to have two places to cruise. So, we  started a once a month cruise night at the Jet Drive In. It was a fun time.

All the car shows at this time were pre-1949, and besides the cruise nights, there was nothing for the 1950's cars to participate in. They wanted to get together too and there were quite a few customs out there besides Rich and his friends.

So, in 1981 Rich started the West Coast Kustoms. He thought he would end up with about 30 members max. These guys wanted to cruise together because they all had a common interest in "Kustoms". Rich would plan something and they would all caravan together to places like Palm Springs, Los Angeles, etc.

One day, Rich received a call from a guy named Max Skirka. He and Gary Minor had heard of the club and wanted to join. Rich said OK, and the membership continued to grow. Rich had club plaques made. The first 25 said "West Coast Kustoms So. Cal".

Membership kept growing as guys from Northern California joined, as well. Rich had to have another 25 plaques made, but these read "West Coast Kustoms" and he thought that it would be cool to have a get together for all the members from both northern and southern California.

Rich was a member of KKOA, Kustom Kemps of America. He wrote to their president, Jerry Titus, explaining that he was thinking of putting on a car show or two. He asked him if he would come to California and help. Mr. Titus didn't think the time was right, and it would be a few years before he would consider it. Rich didn't want to wait.

During the summer of 1982, he got out a map and decided to pick an area halfway between Los Angeles and the San Francisco Bay Area. Then he wrote to several of the towns Chamber of Commerce offices, explaining what he wanted to do. He received only one reply, from the town of Paso Robles. Their Chamber of Commerce thought that Lake Nacimiento, just outside of town would be a place that would be of interest to us and gave us the name of a contact person. So, sight unseen and just a phone call away, Rich started to plan. He called the contact person and was told that they would reserve the whole "North Shore" for us. So, we picked our dates of September 18th and 19th, 1982

for our first event. As to why and how this date was picked, I do not know and guess I never will.

News traveled fast. One weekend before the show, Rich got a call from Joe Bailon inviting him to his home for a BBQ. Joe said that he had heard about our get together and he and Gene Winfield wanted to talk to Rich about it. Rich had never met either of these guys, but thought that it was pretty cool that they were interested and was really looking forward to talking to them. It just wasn't my thing back then, so Rich took a friend.

Rich came home all pumped up. There had been a whole bunch of guys there he told me, but it was nobody I had ever heard about or knew. Besides Joe Bailon and Gene Winfield, there was Steve Stanford (sporting the hairdo of the time, an "afro" ... Wow, wasn't he the cat's meow!) Over the years, we became pretty good friends with Steve.

There were guys from different car magazines like Eric Rickman, aka "Hot Rod Rick". I wish now that I had paid

more attention so I could remember more about who was there that day, but unfortunately, I wasn't really interested back then.

Rich said that the main topic of conversation was about the upcoming get together in Paso Robles. It was really generating a lot of interest with the custom guys.

Along comes the big weekend and on Friday morning Rich leaves with our youngest son, Joe. He is leading the caravan in his cool 1941 Chevy pickup, now chopped, to Paso Robles. I had to stay behind and work until our drive in closed. Finally, at 11:00 p.m., my daughter's boyfriend drove me to Riverside to catch the Greyhound bus. This bus would take me to Los Angeles where I would transfer to the bus bound for Paso Robles. All the stories you hear about bus stations are true ... dirty, smelly and big. Having

to go to the Los Angeles bus terminal did not set well with me. Lucky for me I did see a person I recognized from town. (When you have a small business in town, everybody looks familiar.) She was going to

San Luis Obispo, happy for the company, and knew just where we should go. (Unless there have been some big changes, I will probably never go to the Los Angeles bus depot again.) She talked all the way to San Luis Obispo. So,

I didn't get much rest until she got off the bus, about 45 minutes before arriving in Paso.

I finally reached Paso Robles at 6:00 a.m. on Saturday morning. The Greyhound bus station at that time was locat-ed on Spring St. just south of the Paso Robles Inn. The sun was just coming up and I walked over to the inn. Our room was located in the front, facing the street. As I was knocking on the door of our room, a whistle went off. I guess to alert the little town that it was 6:00 a.m. and time to wake up. It startled me and made me jump. Little did I know, but it was really telling me that this was going to be the day that would change our lives and the town of Paso Robles forever.

Joe Moreno was in town before anyone. He went down to the local paper and told them what was going on, hoping to get himself with his cool 1950 Merc's picture in the paper. Leave it to him to think of that!

We get all ready to go and Joe says he wants to lead the way. So, off we go. We come to a split in the road and Joe goes to the left, but we just stopped and waited. Rich said Joe would be back in a few minutes when he realizes that he went the wrong way. Sure enough, he was and to this day we still give him a bad time and tease him about this.

As we came to the lake, we looked around. Now, mind you, we made all of our arrangements by phone and the man we spoke with said we could have the whole North Shore. Sounded impressive, I thought. Well it sure wasn't what we expected! It was all dirt, rocks, and a boat landing. Oh well, "We will make it work" was the mantra for the day … and we did.

So, I set up at the entrance with a little card table and did registration and Rich did what he did best... talk. We used to have a little joke about the brown spots in our lawn. They were there because Rich stood there talking so long that the sun couldn't get to that spot.

The first show drew about 80 plus customs and one red street rod. Nobody had ever seen that many chopped Mercs in the same place and half of them were in primer. The first participants included Gene Winfield, Joe Bailon, Rod Powell, Sam Foose, Lee Pratt, Joe Moreno, Ron Brooks, and many others. (I know that I am forgetting many more but it has been a long time and back then I didn't read all those little car magazines like the guys did.)

However, I recently heard a story about a young man of about 16 who came to that first event. He lived in Solvang and his father had told him not to come and drive his car out of town. But, kids being kids he didn't listen to his dad and figured if he showed up his dad wouldn't yell at him in front of everyone. Well, that young man was "Chip" Foose. Little did we know then, that the young man from Solvang would become the famous builder, designer, TV personality, and first class guy that he is.

Another story from the first event is about Lee Pratt. He drove his Chevy to Paso all the way from Iowa and really enjoyed the weekend. He told Rich that the only problem was the boat didn't come to the North Shore often enough so he could use the rest room located across the lake. There was a boat that came and took people across the lake to a restaurant and store. Poor Lee wasn't aware there was a restroom located right near the boat landing. Sometimes, we still bring that up in conversation when we see him.

The first event was also the start of the Hall of Fame for West Coast Kustoms. Joe Bailon and Gene Winfield were our first inductees. These were also the only two plaques given out since this was just a get together. We just

wanted to enjoy each other's company, share ideas, and check out each other's rides. That Saturday night, on our first cruise, we went to the A&W on Spring St.

The next year we decided to try the Casa De Fruita at Hollister. We even had a small hall and Rod Powell's' brother, Bo, and his band played music for us. That year we inducted Bill Cushenberry and Ed "Big Daddy" Roth into our Hall of Fame. Casa de Fruita was okay, but it still didn't feel right. We had to keep looking.

For our third year, we did a three day show, September 14, 15 and 16. WOW, can you believe it? We decided to go back to Paso Robles. We had found Sherwood Park, a nice place on the outside of town. That year our special guests included Joe Wilhelm, Frank De Rosa, Rod Powell, Ed "Big Daddy" Roth, Bill Cushenberry, Dick Dean, and Eric "Hot Rod Rick" Rickman. What a line up! Sadly, three of these great guys have passed on.

Rich just knew that Paso Robles was the place. On Sunday, Jim Sanders, from the Paso Robles Chamber of Commerce, came out to the park during the award ceremony, presented Rich with the key to the city, and thanked us for being here. So, we continued to have our shows at Sherwood Park. He invited us to bring the show downtown to the city park across from the Paso Robles Inn, but Rich wasn't all that interested. We liked Sherwood Park.

At the same time as our car show, there was a bicycle show being held at the fairgrounds. We had had some problems with the bicyclists coming out to Sherwood Park to see our cars. They were not too careful with their bicycles around the cars. Rich felt that if we moved into town, the problem would get worse. It didn't matter if a car was painted or in primer, he didn't want to have to worry about bicycles falling against any of our cars. He also felt that the park would not be big enough. He just didn't want a bunch of spectators hanging around.

Mr. Sanders knew there was a problem with the cars trying to cruise on Friday night. The word was out and every kid, father, cousin, and brother was cruising. Some were not behaving themselves, either. So, Mr. Sanders asked if he could get the street closed for just our group to cruise whether we would we consider moving our event downtown. That clinched it! Around this time is when we changed our date from September to Memorial Day weekend. Rich felt that if it was on a holiday weekend then people would have an easier time remembering the date.

As it turned out, downtown was great! On that first weekend, the stores and restaurants were overwhelmed with all of the new people in town eating and shopping. During those first few years, the restaurants ran out of food because they just weren't prepared for it all. The downtown was happy and we were happy. It was nice for the ladies to have a place close by for shopping. They didn't seem to resent being dragged to a car show with nothing to do but sit. During the afternoon, there was also a winery bus that would come, pick people up, and take them on a tour of the local wineries. Unfortunately, that ended a few years ago.

So many people over the years have felt like they were

going to a family reunion and it is so true. I know if it wasn't for West Coast Kustoms, we would never have met so many wonderful people. And we meet new friends every year. Maybe we should just have called it "West Coast Kustoms Family Reunion".

I do know that West Coast Kustoms would not be where it is today without our loyal friends whose hard work over

the years has made it possible for the event and the club to continue.

It's not just me and now my family and friends who work hard, it's Ken Smith and his wife Jan. They are my right arm or my left brain or something. I can honestly say that if it wasn't for Ken doing the awards, creating forms and printing flyers, making lists and more lists, I could not keep everything on track. It's Ken who keeps reminding me about what to do. I am so grateful to have him and Jan for friends.

Then I have my West Coast Kustom Reps. I want to thank them for all their hard work. I know that I am not the easiest person to deal with. There are so many people to thank for the last 25 years. I want you all to know how much I care.

So, when you see me walking and not looking stressed, look for Ken Smith. He's the one stressing, so tell him thanks for the memories.

Hot Rod Lincoln

by Bob Davidson

In all the years that I was in the auto body industry, I repaired a lot of cars and met a lot of people. Because I love cars and people, it was always a thrill for me. In the beginning, I worked for what had been a one-man shop. I would come in to sand and mask the cars, and the guy that owned the shop would come in and spray them at night. We'd get some cars from off the car lots to repair and make a living. Over time, it grew and grew and grew to where it became one of the largest collision companies in the area by far. He became very successful and very wealthy. For me, it was just one of the stepping stones in life.

I met lots of interesting people at that shop. One day, in about 1987, an older couple came in and got an estimate on their late model Nova. As I'm writing up their estimate, the gentleman says to me, "That's a '30 Model A up on the wall there, isn't it?" He was pointing to a picture behind me that I didn't even know was there. But, it was in a nice frame and everything. I turned around and said, "Oh yeah. Yeah, it sure is."

The old boy was about 70 years old, I would say. His wife was sitting on the couch waiting for him to get his estimate completed and he says, "I've got one of those."

I said, "Oh you do? How cool is that?" He said, "Yeah, I've got a Lincoln motor in it." I chuckled and said, "Oh, like the Hot Rod Lincoln." I rattled it off just like that. He continued, not a bit swayed by my casual response, "Yes, I have the original Hot Rod Lincoln."

I couldn't believe what he was saying and asked, "Did you write the song?" "Oh yes," he replied, "a long time ago."

I asked, "Where's the car at?"

"Well, we're retiring in McKenna and we rented a trailer there. We've got a metal garage down there and I have all my stuff in there. It's in there, too."

Having a hard time buying into his statements, I said, "Can we come and see it?"

He says, "Yeah, when I bring my car in you can give me a ride home."

So, I called my friend, Walt Kaplan, who was really into music and asked who wrote the song "Hot Rod Lincoln". He knew it just like that and replied "Charlie Ryan."

I shouted, "Are you kidding? He just left here."

He asked, "Are you kidding? Where's the car?" and I went on to tell him about the guy and his wife and the car out in McKenna.

About the time I hung up with Walt, my buddy Dick Page came in the door and I told him the story and said, "He's bringing his late model car in for repairs on Monday and I'm going to give him a ride back home. He says he'll take me down and show me the car. You wanna go with me?"

Dick quickly responded, "Absolutely!"

On Monday, Dick was at the shop right on time and I introduced him to Charlie when he came in. We took Charlie back to his place, anxious to make a historical barn find. Walking down to the metal building, the anticipation swelled in our hearts and minds. I'll never forget the moment when Charlie opened that big old door of the building and I looked in. There, in the dark recesses, the sunlight dancing over the front grill shell, motor, and faded red cowl, sat The Hot Rod Lincoln. I asked if it even ran and Charlie told me that it hadn't been started or driven in many years.

We walked around the car, looking it over. It had mattresses on it, pigeons flying in and out of it, and junk all over the place. I looked at  Dick and said, "Wouldn't it be awesome if we could restore this thing and bring it back to life?"

Ol' Charlie looked at me said, "Oh, I can't afford that."

I smiled and said, "Wait a minute now, Charlie. I'll get it done and it won't cost you a dime. If you have any other parts ..." Well, he had the taillights off the Lincoln real handy and some other stuff in boxes and as he looked around, he told me the story right then and there.

Many people have heard the song "Hot Rod Lincoln". It has been recorded numerous times by various artists and will always be part of the fabric of early Rock and Roll or Rockabilly music. What a majority of the casual listening public doesn't know is the history of the car behind the song or that there even was a real car.

While there have been quite a few things written about Charlie Ryan and the Hot Rod Lincoln, they don't always say the same thing. But, here's what Charlie told me ...

Charlie had a band and they rode around in a 1947 Lincoln Zephyr from one gig to the next gig. After the guys were done playing, they'd throw their instruments up on the roof of it and head out to their next stop. Charlie was always writing lyrics down. He'd sit in the backseat, sipping on a beer or two, scribbling lyrics and humming new tunes, while they drove to the next venue. They did quite a bit of this routine after their gigs, Charlie writing songs, some of which were about the Lincoln, not putting the year of the car or nothing down, just lyrics about a Hot Rod Lincoln. The song never seemed to want to be completed and this went on and on for quite some time. That all changed one night.

On one outing, they were going from New Mexico into Texas, then into Oklahoma, and finally up the coast of California, where they rolled the Lincoln one night. Everyone got out safely, but the car was destroyed. They took it to a wrecking yard that Charley's dad owned because it was near Bakersfield, California.

The Lincoln body was taken off the chassis and a Model A body was put on it. This is when the unfinished song took a new direction. Charlie started to add the lyrics about the Model A and it all started to come together.

The 12-cylinder engine was in its original place as he went on with his lyrics and the "new voice" of it. When some of the lyrics in the song refer to a Cadillac passing them by, it had actually been the '47 Lincoln in some of the original lyric lines. The references to the Model A and the Cadillac came after they had rolled the Lincoln.

So, he told me this whole story about how they finally finished the song and a record company immediately wanted him to record it. Well, he did. Johnny Bond recorded it, too, and it got on the Hit Parade at about the same time with both recordings. Charlie was an artist himself, but Johnny Bond was Gene Autry's sidekick and he wanted to do the song in his own style. That recording went right up to the top immediately and drew all kinds of attention.

Once in a while, Charlie would take the car and park it outside a gig like a Grange Hall where he was performing with his band, the Rough Riders, to draw attention and pull the people inside. It wasn't the car we see today or the quality you expect to see today in a promotional car. In fact, other than a few people that saw the car at those venues that Charlie and the band played and displayed the car, most people listening to the music on the radio or records only thought of the car as whatever their mind conjured up.

So, as Dick and I stood in the garage, surveying the car, the restoration played out in our minds. We evaluated what was there and what was going to be needed, as well as who we might be able to get involved.

This restoration was our way of helping Charlie, a living legend in the mind of many, and preserving the car that had become so iconic… to those that knew it even existed. For others, this would begin a completely new era for the song, the car, and for Charlie and Ruthie Ryan.

Charlie was certainly agreeable, but he wanted to know why this wasn't costing him anything. We reassured him that it was our way of giving back and so, he turned the car over to me and let us do our thing. Charlie just didn't realize the basic irresistible urge and the ultimate satisfaction that an old hot-rodder could get from being involved in the restoration of a car of this legendary status.

Everyone we approached and asked for help was anxious to get involved and all of the time, materials, and funds were donated. From new whitewall tires to the paint, it was all for Charlie and it was all given freely with nothing expected in return. We didn't take or ask for anything. Because of the nature of the build and the excitement that it generated, there was a lot of good will floating around and so, there was a lot of attention given to the companies that were involved.

It worked out good. We took it over to Benny Jones. He had a little mechanical garage. His dad was Levie Jones, the racecar driver. So, he had a lot of equipment and Benny got it all when his dad passed away. He got the '47 Zephyr engine fired up in not much time at all. After all those years, it was running. Then, we went and got a hold of other people to donate their talent. Benny had donated his time and resources. Then we started the bodywork, the interior, and the remaining mechanical restoration of the vehicle.

The person that did the interior, Don McCloud, got credit for the upholstery work he did on the side. Winchell's did the bodywork at their body shop on Pacific Avenue. The hood, as it was, needed to be re-fabbed and so we cut and shaped a hood so it would go from the cowl to the grill shell. We also made a smooth top for it out of tin.

Charley still had the Model A taillights on it and so, we removed them and took round '49 Lincoln taillights

 and mounted them in the fenders, giving it a real neat look. The rear bumpers we put on were from a '48 Lincoln. We got a van company to donate a spare tire cover that they put on the custom vans and I painted and lettered it to look like the 45 record label of the song.

We gave it new hubcaps and put brand new white wall tires on it, which it hadn't had before, and the man that donated the tires got credit for his tire company. Some of the things from the original Lincoln went onto the Model

A body that he had wanted to incorporate, but had never done. He still had all of the pieces and parts and we made a lot of it work.

We put the Lincoln dashboard in it and I lettered notes and lyrics on it. On the left side of the steering column, above the gauges, I put "Son, you're gonna drive to drinkin' ..." and on the other side, just to the right of the clock, I finished with "if you don't stop drivin' that Hot Rod Lincoln". The chrome and stainless on the dash shined like new and the lettering really made it all pop. It got a nice new leather interior to replace the original old ragged ass seat that was in there and other things we could to make it a show car.

There are pictures of all of it being built and Rod and Custom magazine wrote an article to show the pictures and tell the story. It was just amazing. Charlie and his wife were blown away with all of the attention and they couldn't believe what was going on.

To upgrade the car and make it more safe and durable than what they had thrown together back in the late '40s, we took care of any mechanical work. The '47 Zephyr motor wasn't rebuilt, but it got suspension and brake work and whatever else was needed. It was all done right, with no corners cut. Charlie and Ruthie Ryan were amazed at how the car turned out.

The redone Hot Rod Lincoln made its debut at Rock the Dock, which is down on the waterfront in Tacoma. They put the car up above and Charlie performed with a band that he had put together out of the local union. There was a car show inside, as well. It was an awesome event to introduce everybody to Charlie and the freshened up Hot

Rod Lincoln. A lot of people said, "You duplicated the old hot rod!" We explained that THIS was the original Hot Rod Lincoln and NOT a reproduction. Even with all of the publicity that was floating around, there were a lot of people that didn't know there was an original Hot Rod Lincoln.

They took the car to some of the big car shows like Good Guys. They bought brand new jackets to go with the theme and at 72 years old, Charlie started to perform again on a regular basis. The magazines got a hold of this and everything started to grow. Charlie never got so much attention in his life.

Charlie and Ruthie belonged to ASCAP. He told me all about how the songwriter is paid when their song is performed or when the record is produced. That's where he got his money and when Charlie and that Hot Rod Lincoln got debuted around this area, the radio stations were playing "Hot Rod Lincoln" continuously. It was unbelievable. Every channel, every station, every television was all over it. There was all of this excitement just off what we created from the restoration and having that car available for the people to actually look at and see.

The Ryans wrote countless letters and cards, thanking all of the people that brought a new life to him and his wife by bringing the car to the way it was originally meant to be. They had never had the time or money to do it, because they were so busy trying to make a living.

He got on the television show Nashville Now and the car was rolled out on the stage while Charlie performed. He never had done anything like that before and it was the first time the car was ever shown to the general public on national television. The magazine coverage was amazing, as well.

They had moved to Spokane to live after the car was

done. He was asked to join the Dukes Car Club and, of course, he was thrilled. In 1990, Rod and Custom magazine did their story on the Hot Rod Lincoln, including pictures of before, during, and after the restoration. Some of the photographs in that article were sent to them by some of the workers and, of course, I gave them all the pictures that I had developed from a little snapshot camera that we were using at the time.

Charlie and Ruthie wrote a lot of songs. If you listen to one of their tapes, there's Side Car Sally and a lot of others. Ruthie was a heck of a writer, too.

Charlie never had a lot of money and he was getting up there in years. The song "Hot Rod Lincoln" might live forever, but Charlie knew he wouldn't. So, Charlie and Ruthie gave the car to a car collector in Chicago in return for his promise to take care of Ruthie during her remaining years. Whether she was in a nursing home or wherever, he was going to pay the bills in return for that car. Charlie passed away of a heart attack in 2008. He and Ruthie had been married for over 70 years.

Apparently, Ruthie has passed away, because I haven't heard from her in quite some time. I used to get greeting cards from her every Christmas, but she was getting older and older.

The Hot Rod Lincoln was the star Hot Rod of the 60th Detroit Autorama in 2012 and Barrett Jackson states that the car was sold at auction in January 2013 at The Scottsdale Barrett Jackson Auction for $106,700.

While Charlie and Ruthie are gone, the car is still out there somewhere and I hope in loving hands. The song, with its iconic lyrics, is still on the airwaves and will live in the hearts of many forever.

The Legend Lives On

by Ky Michaelson

Things that other people can do without seem to be the things I can't live without and I have found many of my greatest treasures participating in one of my favorite pastimes, swap meet rummaging.

One brisk September morning in 2004, I found myself in Davenport, Iowa for the Antique Motorcycle Club of America swap meet. While digging through the mountains of other people's junk, I was surprised to see "it" sitting there. Perched on top of a milk crate was the most beautiful "for sale" sign my eyes had ever seen. There it stood in all its glory, stopping me dead in my tracks, a 1912 Michaelson Minneapolis motorcycle engine. This is what I would consider to be my Holy Grail and I would do anything to get that engine in my hands. I introduced myself to the dealer that had the engine for sale and told him about my family's connection to that engine.

He shared with me that many years ago he had bought an old Flanders Motorcycle. Because he wanted the Flanders to be more correct, he swapped out the Michaelson motor for an original Flanders engine. The best part of the deal was he told me that the Minneapolis motor ran like a top before he took it out of the bike.

I would have paid any amount of money to be the new owner of that priceless engine, but he was only asking $3,500. I held my engine like a proud papa, with a grin that reached from ear to ear, as I walked through the exit doors and I thought of how my grandfather had once done the same. Over the years, I have been asked "Why don't you buy one of the old motorcycles that your family built?" I

 would always respond the same, "That was my family's history. I make my own history".

But, I am very proud of my heritage, and the many accomplishments that my family achieved while they manufactured the Michaelson and the Minneapolis Motorcycles. Now all of a sudden, I owned a part of the Michaelson history and I started thinking about what I would do with that engine. My first thought was that I would build a copy of the 1915 Michaelson three wheel Motorcycle known as the "Tri Car". But, when I was out for "Speed Week" at the Booneville Salt Flats, one of my fellow racers told me that they had just finished shooting a film called "The World's Fastest Indian". This film is about the life story of Burt Munro and it is an incredible movie.

Over the years, I have read a number of articles about Burt and his 1920 Indian Scout motorcycle. This guy knew how to work with his hands. He was innovative and with very few tools, he managed to make his own pistons and many other components for his bike. With the odds against him, he set many speed records with his 1920 Indian, including one run over 200 mph. When I went to see Burt's film, I sat thinking how I should honor my family by building a streamline motorcycle using the Michaelson motor I had just acquired. I dreamt of seeing it on the Bonneville Salt Flats. What a great tribute to six generations of Michaelson thrill seekers that would be. I would name the motorcycle "The Legend Lives On".

At first, I thought this project was going to be a piece of cake. Then reality hit me. How do I build a streamline motorcycle when they did not even have streamliner bikes back then? So, my challenge was not to restore the bike but to create a completely new one with a mix of present and past. That way, I could incorporate my style of building and still feature the 1912 engine as the "star" of the bike.

I began with building the frame out of 4130 chrome moly tubing and bent up the lightweight frame rails. The frame was about 10 feet long and would give the bike a long sleek look. I used an unconventional ball-bearing center hub to steer the bike. The motorcycle was only going to be used on a straight racecourse, so I didn't have to worry about its limited steering radius. I added a shock to the steering arm to help cut down on any wobbling and decided to build the handle bars out of 6061 T-6 aluminum. These are very unique looking handlebars that took a lot of machine work to get them to look the way I wanted them. I also added a quick release on the handle bars to I could take them off easily by just pushing a pin. This was

necessary so when doing maintenance I could easily remove the body off the chassis without spending a lot of time removing the handlebars.

I built the body out of 3003 H14 aluminum. Many years ago I bought a spinner off an airplane at a swap meet and that spinner made the perfect nose cone on the bike. I fabricated some aluminum to cover up the hole where the prop was originally located. The nose cone went to a friend of mine, Dan Fate, who had the tools to make two pieces with louvers on them to cover up the other two holes on the nose cone. Now, the bike started to take on an art deco look. This got me thinking about what else could be done to follow through with this look.

I always liked the way the old fighter planes looked with their boxy looking windshields all pop riveted together. So, I cut out a piece of cardboard to use as a template. I liked my first prototype, so I went ahead and made it out of aluminum. I added Plexiglas to the frame work and the button head screws gave a nice contemporary look. I really liked the way the bike was headed

Next, I was going to take on building the seat. I got to thinking that in recent years most of the things I have been building have had rockets on them. That night while lying in bed, I remembered that many years ago, sometime in the early 60's, I had bought a bunch of aluminum nose cones. They came from the Honeywell surplus store in Minneapolis and were off ballistic missiles. Being the pack rat that I am, I still had them stored in the back room of my shop. I used the curved section of the nose cone by cutting out the top of the seat with a saber saw. I made the sidepieces using a sheet metal roller and did a little shaping using a hammer and a dolly. A 4-speed transmission and clutch set-up out of a 1960 BSA would make it easy to work on. I bent up a real slick looking exhaust pipe out of stainless steel.

In February, at the annual Super Bowl party at my house, I invited many of my antique motorcycle buddies. I surprised them all by starting the bike up for the first time. My friend, Mike Wagner, took on the honors of kicking it over. We shot a little ether into the carburetor, and after a couple dozen hard kicks, the motor came to life. It sounded absolutely incredible. I was a proud papa again. The crowd was as enthusiastic I was.

With all of the mechanical and fabrication work done, I disassembled the whole bike and we then took all of the aluminum parts to Joe Deters Metal Finishing. I had him polish and chrome everything. All the body parts and frame went to my good friends, Bruce and Kelly, who own a company called Wizard Custom Studios, St. Croix Airbrushing. Bruce had the frame sand blasted and painted it gloss black. I had a real hard time deciding what color to paint the bike until Bruce showed me some paint that he had sitting on the shelf that came from the House of Color. The paint was called Blue Blood and I have never seen a nicer red. He applied several coats of the red and then a clear coat.

Kelly did a great job air brushing the Michaelson logo on both sides of the bike. Mike Hovland pinstriped the bike and for an added extra touch, he then put the number 17 in gold leaf on the side of the seat. I picked 17 because over the years that number has been very good to me. The black leather upholstery was done by Jennie Bloedorn.

After a week of assembling and detailing, the bike was finally finished. I am very proud of how the bike turned out and for my perseverance of six long years in designing and building it. I named the bike "The Legend Lives On" because of the family history passed on to me.

When I pass on, I am sure my family will be as proud as I am of this Michaelson Motorcycle. My son, Buddy, and I entered the bike in the 56th annual G.S.T.A. Rod and Custom Spectacular and it won first prize in its class. Buddy was a big part of the reason I built this bike. I wanted him to see the process, but even more so I wanted him to carry on the tradition of Michaelson innovators. The Michaelson Legend Lives On … in name and in spirit.

Charlie's Packard

by Clayton Stott

Some time ago, I received a call from a fellow member of the Gig Harbor Cruisers. He wanted to know how to locate a car that had been sold to the LeMay Car Collection. His friend, Charlie, had been his high school band teacher in Tacoma many years ago. When Charlie was in his late 20's, he purchased a 1927 Packard at an auction. At that time, his Packard was a modified tow truck.

Charlie was not one to be dissuaded. He found a four-door body to fit the frame, engine, and wheelbase and over several years, Charlie painted the body, installed new upholstery and did work on the engine, brakes and transmission. As his family grew, the Packard became a luxury he could no longer afford. He eventually sold the car to Harold E. LeMay.

As Charlie's life rolled on, he often wondered what had happened to "his" Packard. The curiosity was the topic of conversations with anyone who would listen. Eventually, my friend, Rich decided to see what he could do to help Charlie in his quest. They started with the new LeMay Museum, America's Car Museum in Tacoma. The staffers there were not able to help them locate the Packard.

Eventually, Rich called me and we thought about how best to track down the car. As a volunteer at Le May at Marymount, I had access to a wealth of institutionalized collective knowledge about the history of much of the Harold and Nancy LeMay collection. In one of my conversations with another docent, a light glimmered and he thought he remembered Charlie's Packard. That led to other conversations with other docents who also contributed more information.

It turned out that Charlie's Packard was sold at auction through America's Car Museum. At some point subsequent to that sale, Doug LeMay purchased the car back. From there, the trail became very murky, very quickly. Eventually, it was discovered that the Packard was at another off-site LeMay location.

A few phone calls later and a determination was made about the exact whereabouts of Charlie's Packard. Bear in mind this odyssey took several months. On the appointed day, Rich and I drove to Tacoma to take Charlie to lunch. He had no idea that we had located his beloved '27 Packard.

After lunch, as we were preparing to take Charlie back to Tacoma, I mentioned that I needed to go to LeMay at Marymount Academy to "pick up some papers". When I mentioned LeMay, Charlie came alive. He told me, in great detail, about how he had sold his Packard to Harold LeMay and how he had been looking for information about it for many years. The three of us boarded Rich's car and headed for Marymount Academy with Charlie excitedly talking a mile-a-minute about the '27 Packard.

When we pulled into the main parking lot, Charlie  could not wait to get out of Rich's car and inside the facility. He had no idea what we had planned for him. We went to the registration area, where several people met Charlie. He could not help but tell them the story of the connection between Harold LeMay and his prized Packard.

After a few minutes, we travelled to one of the out buildings on the LeMay Marymount campus. Charlie walked through the door and there, literally in a spotlight, sat his 1927 Packard. Several volunteers were standing nearby to watch the spectacle. Those same volunteers had lovingly transported his car from a remote off-site LeMay location, delivered it to the building, and then lovingly detailed it.

Though there are many rules about not touching cars in the LeMay Collection, this case was different. We encouraged Charlie to sit in the car and tell us how it felt. The first thing he noticed was that it was a tight fit between the seat back and steering wheel. Over the years, the car must have shrunk. After a careful inspection of the cockpit and dash, Charlie got out and provided us with a living history of the car.

He told us how he had removed the tow truck body and replaced it with a four-door clip. We learned about how he painted the car, including the pin striping. The tops to both battery covers and the hood ornament didn't look like

they were original Packard  issued parts and Charlie explained that he could not afford to buy battery box covers or an authentic hood ornament, so he made sand impressions from borrowed original parts and then made aluminum sand castings from those impressions.

Clearly, to those who were there, this was a very special reuniting of a man and his dream. Doug LeMay and other LeMay family members came out and helped Charlie celebrate the event and he spent about two hours reminiscing about his prize '27 Packard. We took him on an abbreviated tour of the LeMay Collection at Marymount and then returned him to his home in Tacoma.

That happened on a Thursday afternoon. It was a great day for Charlie, Rich, and for the wonderful volunteers at LeMay Family Collection.

The following Monday, I received a call from Charlie's wife. Her conversation was moving. She was thankful that Charlie had had an opportunity to visit his old and beloved friend; his '27 Packard. She then told me that Charlie had passed away over the weekend following his visit to LeMay.

I am honored to serve as a docent at The LeMay Family Collection at Marymount in Tacoma, Washington. This  unification between Charlie and his Packard would never have happened if someone (Rich) had not reached out, looking to help Charlie. Moreover, it never would have happened were it not for the wonderful volunteers and the LeMay family who took the time to sort through the collection to find one very special car for a very special individual.

Model A in the Barn

by Dale Erickson

As a farm boy growing up in the 1950's, I was driving tractors at age 11 and trucks in the fields and on farm roads at 13. Getting a driver's license was a major goal and was accomplished the instant I turned 16. But, my parents were of the opinion that no 16 year old should have their own car and so I was relegated to a "limited" use of the family sedan.

It did not take too long however, for a slight philosophical change in their attitude to occur. They suddenly realized that they no longer had to get in the car and come get me from after school sports and other such activities, because I was legally able to drive. I just needed some form of transportation. It was agreed that I could buy '31 Model A Coupe that was advertised for sale in a city 35 miles away for $150. Dad and I drove down there and purchased the car and I drove it home.

It did not take long for the engine to start making some loud obnoxious noises and my farmer father said he would NOT deal with any Babbitt bearing issues. I was able to order a rebuilt engine out of the Montgomery Ward catalog and when it arrived, my dad helped me exchange motors and life was good.

That little coupe took me to school every day and to friend's houses for many of the things young boys need to do. It took my friends and me, just country boys who loved the outdoors, up driving in the hills. During hunting season, we would take it into the backcountry and into the snow. We would pass four-wheel drive pickups that had reached their limit and had only jeep tracks ahead of us. It actually took my schoolteacher mom to work a couple of mornings when it was well below zero and the Model A was the only thing on the place that would start.

When I graduated from high school in 1962, my first job in the local sawmill produced the money needed to buy a much more stylish automobile, a 1960 Chevrolet convertible. My younger brother, and then my younger sister, used the Model A the same way I did through their school years. My sister recalls having what seemed like twenty friends piled in and on that car to run down to the only store in our little town during lunchtime. She graduated in 1968 and like her older brothers before her, was allowed to buy her own car. She pulled the Model A into the back corner of Dad's hay barn and turned off the key.

When I got back from the service, I knew it would be awhile before I was in a position to do anything with it. But, since it owed me nothing and the storage was free, I just let her sit. I drained the old antifreeze, removed the battery, and went to the farm tractor diesel tank and got 3 or 4 gallons of diesel. I removed the spark plugs and dumped in all they would take. I then removed the oil filler cap and

 poured diesel down it until it overflowed.

The car spent the next 42 years in one barn or another until I retired in 2010. I rented a trailer and winched the car out of the barn it had spent the last dozen years in and hauled it home. I changed the oil in the engine, transmission, and rear end. Then, I bought a new

battery, four spark plugs, and five gallons of gas. After I took the Tillotson carb apart and sprayed carb cleaner all over it, I put it back together with the same gaskets. It start-ed up as if it had been running the previous week.

I took my daughter for a ride around the block, but since it seemed that only one front brake was working, the ride was slow and short. So, wanting to be involved, she helped me get one of the rear brakes working. That allowed me to take my wife of 30 years, who had never been in the car, for a ride up around the lake. When we got home, I pulled it into the garage and started a frame off restoration.

Since the engine had run and sounded so good, I just pulled it out of the car and set it aside. I knew that it should come out pretty easy and be able to be worked on later. I could then use my limited budget on things that the car needed most. I ended up with the frame on sawhorses. Everything was sandblasted, repaired, replaced, straightened, and/or welded up.

Patch panels were welded in and dents hammered out. I took the bodywork to the limit of my skill level and then took it to a custom shop owned and operated by a friend of my son-in-law. I got the body and the fenders back looking perfect.

My goal, when I started, was to have a 10 and 10 car. "It looks good from 10 feet away at 10 mph". Even though I had been more meticulous than planned with the body and paint, I knew it could never be a "concours quality" car because of all the reproduction parts. It has 16-inch wheels and aftermarket sealed beam headlights, both of which were on it when I bought it.

It is painted a color that was supposed to be one of the original colors per the paint supplier, but is more of a  brown. It is, however, a color we love and sets us slightly apart from the rest. It is straight and with a quality finish that is better than a lot of cars in its crowd. It took me 11 months from the trailer ride home until I drove it on its first tour with our Model A Club. We have put 2500 miles on it since. The engine still runs great after all of these years and we still enjoy every mile we drive.

The Human Fly

by Ky Michelson

In 1977, I was contracted to build a rocket-powered motor-cycle capable of jumping over 27 buses. The jump was to take place in the Montreal Olympic Stadium as a half-time show for a concert featuring Gloria Gaynor and a number of other disco stars of the 70's. The daredevil rider was Rick Rojatt, otherwise known as The Human Fly.

At the time, Evil Kneivel held the record jump of 13 buses and Rick wanted to beat it badly. Rick's claim to fame at that point in his career was an astonishing stunt he'd performed over the Mojave Desert where he'd wing-walked on a DC-8 and actually made two low flying passes at 250 mph, a nearly impossible feat and truly death-defying. The other very unique thing about this off-the-wall daredevil was that he was never seen out of costume and kept his true identity a secret by wearing a red mask and a white cape identical to the comic book action hero.

From the moment I met this guy, I was convinced he was an accident looking for a place to happen, especially when he told me he wanted to attempt 36 buses. I managed to convince him otherwise when we discussed the fact that in order to do something that remarkable, he'd have to hit the jump ramp at well over 100 mph and continue to burn the rocket a couple more seconds after take off. I explained that it was definitely possible, but the fact remained that acceleration of that magnitude in such a small area would launch him head-first through the concrete pillar at the opposite end of the arena.

That conversation resulted in his finally accepting the challenge for 27 instead. He'd still have to travel at 80 mph and it wasn't that there wouldn't be a crash, for I was certain there would be. It was just a matter of how bad it would be by the time he reached our nets and a huge airbag we'd have set up. I knew the decrease in speed and thrust would make a huge difference and felt we could pull this one off with minimal damage to the bike or to Rick (hopefully).

The guy was determined and since my business at the time was working with stunt people, daredevils, and people with death wishes, I remained intrigued and as optimistic as possible, praying I wouldn't fall witness to the hand of death "swatting" the Human Fly. I became even more concerned when I received a phone call from an insurance broker, Bruce McCaw, who called to thank me, saying I was responsible for throwing a lot of business his way. When I asked him what he meant by that, he told me he'd just issued a life insurance policy on the Human Fly and that Lee Taylor had been a client of his, as well. That really got me thinking.

As we prepared for this stunt, it soon became obvious that one of the biggest challenges we faced was the space constraint in the arena. There was no room to accelerate to the speed required, so I came up with a plan. I'd build a rocket-powered motorcycle that would sit right at the bottom of the ramp instead of making the usual fast and furious approach. All the Fly would have to do was get on, wave to the crowd, press the button, say a quick prayer, and hang on for dear life!

Rick liked the idea and agreed to try it, so he sent me a brand new 1977 Harley Davidson XL-1000 Sportster, a true black beauty, to build from. I put exactly three miles on it and then the fun began. I yanked out the engine and built two 1,500-lb. thrust hydrogen peroxide rockets, which I mounted one on top of the other, directly underneath the fuel tank. Other than the two polished stainless steel rocket motors hanging off the back of the bike, I left everything else intact, including the headlight and taillight, to make it look completely stock. By the time I finished, this refined machine boasted 6,000 horsepower. In other words, if a guy were to take this thing out to the local drag strip, hold the throttle wide open, and hang on hoping the tires didn't fall right off, he'd be capable of going well over 300 mph in the ¼ mile.

I let Rick know the bike was ready and we delivered it to Montreal. We all met up the day before the big event, delivered all the equipment, and met with the promoters to discuss the plans.

They had hired contractors to put the jump equipment together for us, which I wasn't real happy about, but finally agreed to. We went over the stunt as thoroughly as possible and much to my amazement

Ky with The Human Fly.

Rick didn't want to do any practice runs at all. He just sat on the bike, admiring it, determined to just wait until the time came. I gave him step-by-step detailed instructions on how to operate the rockets and he just took it all in, nodding as I went along. I knew he understood what I was saying, but I hardly slept that night because I was always so safety conscious and typically rehearsed stunts many times before actually performing them. I was uneasy with this particular situation.

Jim Deist, Dar Robinson, and I arrived at the arena bright and early. Much to our surprise, we could clearly see that the blueprints for both the jump and receiving ramps were obviously not adhered to, as there were major flaws in both of them. The jump ramp was much too steep, which would cause the rocket bike to come off it at the wrong angle and stall. I was even more concerned about the receiving ramp, though, as the last ten buses were supposed to be covered by plywood extending to the ramp.

What we found instead was a plywood ramp that was about six feet above the buses, with exposed steel cross members. I told the promoters that their contractors, or whoever it was that built these things, obviously didn't follow the blueprints we'd provided and I was not going to fuel up the rocket bike until major changes were made to the receiving ramp. The whole thing turned into a major ordeal by the time we did our last safety inspection, which forced the show time to change quite a bit.

We watched the entertainment, but there was no sign of the Human Fly anywhere. As intermission approached, we were all really apprehensive, and to be honest I truly couldn't believe my eyes when Rick and his entourage entered the arena. I had secretly been hoping he'd maybe gotten up that morning, looked in the mirror and asked himself, "Do I really want to die? Is this really a good idea? Do I really want to break Evel's record this badly?"

That was not to be, though, and as the promoter announced the stunt and The Human Fly took center stage in full costume, the crowd went absolutely wild. I stood in awe as he hopped on the motorcycle, waved to the crowd, looked over at me, gave the thumbs up, turned on the safety switch, and slowly opened the throttle.

The rocket bike started up the ramp slowly at first and then the Human Fly pinned the throttle wide open. The cloud of smoke was a sight to behold in the nearly pitch dark arena. The super-heated steam shot out the back as the bike climbed up the ramp and instead of launching forward into the air,  went much higher than it should have and nearly straight up. Because of the wrong angle, it stalled when he let off the throttle and the rear end dropped, nearly arching the bike completely backwards as it hit the receiving ramp hard before crashing down on him.

My heart just pounded as I stood there, witnessing the crash of all crash landings right before my eyes. A hush fell over the crowd as we all feared the worst, because it looked like nobody could have possibly survived such a crash landing. We were soon relieved though, when we realized he was actually okay. He'd survived the crash and had broken Evil's record, but not without paying the price. He waved to the crowd as he was carried off on a stretcher, suffering a broken ankle and a couple other injuries.

That jump and my rocket bike went down in the history books and then, as things work out, I lost track of both the Human Fly and the bike. I'm happy to say, however, that this story has a rather unique ending. Even though I had long since gotten over owning that fine machine, I received a call not long ago from a stuntman friend of mine, Bubba, a renowned and darn good motorcycle jumper himself, with some astonishing news.

He told me he had picked up a "Trading Times" magazine while he was in Florida and was dumbfounded when he spotted a motorcycle in it that he could have sworn was my original rocket bike. He gave me the phone number, and I immediately contacted the owner, John Werner, who  attested and confirmed that it was in fact the bike used in that incredible stunt. I told him to name his price; I wanted it back, and BADLY, so he agreed to sell it back to me for $6,500. I sent a good friend of mine down to pick it up and I am pleased and proud to say that it is now resting back in my rocket shop where I built it some 23 years ago.

They had it rebuilt after the crash and it looks as good as new; in great shape. The only thing they changed was to ad a gas tank. I find myself just staring at it frequently and reminiscing back to that history-making event quite often. I'm happy to say that if you ever hear of anybody looking for a bike that can jump 27 buses, I've got just the thing. But, there's one condition. They need to see a psychiatrist first!

I Never Let Go!

by Bill Jackson

When I was a 12-year-old boy growing up in the San Fernando Valley, I had a dream of owning a Hot Rod. It was in the summer of 1948 that I had bought a copy of Hot Rod Magazine and fell in love with one of the featured cars, a '29 roadster. I knew I must have one similar.

When the time came to get a car, I found a track T roadster body that was set up for a Model A frame. The doors were welded shut and it had been cut down for entry over the top. Sadly, this car was never finished and many others that I have owned since have suffered a similar fate.

Then, in 1951, my dream car was found in a Canoga Park used-car lot. It was a '32 Ford roadster. I bought it and took it to a friend of mine who did bodywork. After a few months, we decided the body just wasn't worth the effort to fix. That was a letdown, although I felt that all was not lost, because I still had the chassis and I would put a '29 roadster body on it.

Well, my world crashed in the fall of 1951 when the California Fender Law came into effect. This law was not taken lightly by police departments and driving such a vehicle on the streets guaranteed you a multitude of traffic tickets. My desire to own a fenderless car was still there, but I became a little more amenable to the idea of having fenders on my car.

In 1952, a scrap collector stopped by my folk's house and told me of a '29 roadster body that was for sale in the town of Newhall. I went there and didn't care much for the condition of the roadster, but in an unfinished garage next to it sat a complete '32 Tudor Model B that was all in pieces. I bought it and found that it had been in an accident and

the K member had been bent. The body had not been hurt and so here was a perfect use for the roadster chassis. That was until I thought of all of the problems of registering a Tudor that was supposed to be a roadster.

In late 1953 or early 1954, in Receda, the town in which I lived, there was a chopped Tudor being sold. I thought this would be the perfect set up and so I bought it. Because my body was in much better condition, I put it on the newly acquired frame and used my running gear. Registration was now easy.

I installed hydraulic brakes, a dropped axle, big and littles, used the filled shell and King Bee headlights from the roadster, and removed the parking lights. The final thing was the addition of an early V8 engine with an extremely radical Winfield cam.

I drove it to high school in my senior year. In about December 1954, I had stopped at a stop sign and was accelerating in second gear when I hit a tar patch on a concrete road. One of the rear tires bounced off the road and when it came down, I lost most of the gears in both the transmission and rear end. I was suspicious that it was the rear end that had failed first, so it was time for a stronger one and a general cleanup of the car. In the end, it was not driven again until 2012, but I didn't give up on it.

In 1955, the car was torn down again to the bare frame, by now for about the umpteenth time. I painted the running gear white which was a trend at that time. Then I bought a 1940 rear end and had the driveshaft shortened to fit.

My favorite car running around the Valley in 1955 was a deuce Vicky owned by Edward Babcock. He had not shaved the shell nor removed the parking lights and with a louvered hood amongst other things it has been a major influence on the way my car looks today.  I have just recently located Edward through his brother-in-law and had hoped that he had pictures of it, but alas, there are none.

I had put the engine out of the '32 into a '40 Mercury and sold it. Now, I was looking for a new engine. A friend of mine, Michael Larson, had recently built a full race flathead and had blown a clutch at the Saugus drag strip. This engine had a C&T stroker kit, making it 285 cubic inches. Along with this, it was ported and relieved, had Edelbrock heads, and a three carb manifold, along with a good Iskandarian 400 junior cam, H&C dual coil ignition, aluminum flywheel, and of course, headers.

For some reason, he decided to sell the engine and I bought it. This was to be the engine for the Tudor. My daily driver at the time was a nice clean '40 Ford Standard Coupe and every once in a while the big flathead would find its way into its engine compartment.

I was finally working a full-time job and so I turned my attention to making my car a little nicer. Well, the days of white paint were gone and now chrome was in vogue. I started going to Ford Parts Obsolete on Florence Boulevard in South L.A. almost every weekend to see what had come in during the prior week. I was able to buy all the running gear parts NOS and these I had chromed; even the parts inside the brake drums. Everything under the car was chromed.

I was fortunate enough to know two of the finest people and top fuel drag racers of all time, Ronnie and Jeep Hampshire. They were being noticed early in their racing careers and through them I was able to buy many racing parts for the car, including a new Halibrand quick-change rear axle, Bell racing wheel, and more.

The years went by and I met the woman I would marry in early 1960. Our second date was to the March meet in Formosa California. I had a great time. She, not so much, and I did not go back to drag strip again until the summer of 2010. After we were married, my responsibility was with my family and home, so the car got shoved to the back of the garage. Ten years went by and a divorce meant I had to leave my home. I had no place to go and my parents weren't all that happy about seeing me at their front door, let alone dragging my "old car" with me.

I had no time to figure out what to do with my collection of parts, so they were all given away, including the Halibrand, the big flathead, shelves of early transmission clusters, a full set of decent '32 fenders, and much more.

A few months later, I bought out my ex-wife's equity in the house and moved back in. I was home again, but not able to afford to work on the car for almost another 20 years. The body was put on a rolling rack and the frame hung on the wall during most of those years, a constant reminder of the unfinished work I had been putting off. By the end of the 1980s, I realized that I had to finish it or let it go. I chose to finish it.

I wasn't sure where to start, though. I had been away from the hot rod scene for almost 30 years. I began with the basics and the more time I spent with the project, the more I would learn and remember from my youth. All was going well until the compa-
ny I worked for started
downsizing their work-
force. In 1990, after 34 years
with the same company, I
was looking for a job.

I had often thought of
moving to the Pacific Northwest and believed with the high California home values, I had what I considered sub-stantial equity and with my meager retirement, I felt that move was a possibility. However, in 1990 the value of my house dropped $40,000 and it would take years of retire-ment income to make that up. So, I decided to wait it out and continued to work on the car. Initially, I didn't think it could get worse and I just had to be patient and let values rise again. But, by the end of 1993, the house had dropped in value to about $100,000 less than what it had been when I retired.

On January 17 of 1994, at 4:31 AM, life as I had known it changed. The Northridge earthquake destroyed my house. This caused a complete change in plans. Over the next few years, the house problems were finally solved and I moved to Washington State around 2001. The '32 was not worked on from the time of the earthquake until about 2007.

I took a loan out on my house in Washington and start-ed to think about what to do with the car. I was now in my 70s with little background in building modern hot rods. I knew that if I tried learning to weld, paint with the newer materials, and deal with the closer tolerances of the higher power engines, I would be learning on what would become a very expensive automobile. I found an excellent builder in the form of Bill Duncan and let him and his knowledge finish the job for me. Besides, I just wanted to get it done so I could enjoy it!

To the casual observer, my car will probably look like a nicely done non-period correct black cookie-cutter '32 Tudor, but through the old eyes of this once young 12-year-old boy, I see a lifetime dream having finally come true.

Thanks to all of my many friends for their help and encouragement throughout the years. I never let go of the dream, because I never let go of the car!

Car '54

by Martin DeGrazia

In 1976, I was 17 years old and working in a body shop in north Seattle. I worked five days a week after school, making about $25.00 per week at $2.10 an hour. Out of that $25.00, I would purchase one cassette tape to the likes of Robin Trower, Bob Seeger, Montrose, and Aerosmith. I liked the hard stuff.

My boss had a bunch of '60's Mustangs that he used for loaner cars, one of which was a cool, green '68 Mustang. On a busy Friday afternoon during rush hour, I had to take the '68 Mustang across busy highway 99. At this point, I did not have a car of my own, so I didn't have lot of driving experience. It seemed like it was taking forever to get across and I had to get going. I figured I could go right after the red car slowly poking its way along toward me. As I looked left, the cars coming north were fast approaching. I looked right. I looked left. Frustrated, I gunned it and turned to the right and there to my surprise was a grey Government Issue station wagon right in front of me. There was nothing I could do but watch the collision unfold. It seemed like it took forever, but the impact was imminent and I nailed the other car hard.

So, I got out and made sure the guy in the other car was ok. Thankfully, he was. His government assigned ride didn't do as well, however. I had ruined the driver's side door on the grey wagon. On the Mustang, I managed to destroy the bumper, the fender, and the hood.

My boss didn't take it too well and he wanted me to pay him $165 for the damage to his car. I explained to him it was an accident and he was making a good living off people like me. "No", he said, "What you did was stupid!" He went on to call me every name in the book and then some. Of course, I was fired, but then told me he was going to fire my brother, too. I didn't think firing my brother was right, but as far as me not coming back in… no problem.

Now that I was unemployed, I decided the only thing to do was buy a car of my own. I grabbed my younger brother, Tom. He was the real car guy in the family. I had decided what I wanted was a '62 – '66 Chevy Nova. In my mind, they were cool and could be affordable. But, who am

 I kidding? I just wanted something cooler than my mother's wagon. So, we headed up Highway 99, ironically in my mother's wagon, looking at all the cheap cars. We finally made it to Chuck Olson Chevrolet in north Seattle.

In the back of the lot was this very cool looking, burnt orange, older car. It had one of those windshield sun visors on it and a white top. The chrome bumpers and stainless trim shined brightly and the paint was in excellent condition for its age. There must have been a half dozen people all over that thing as we walked over to take a closer look.

It was a cool car, but I had only $400.00 to spend and this would surely be more than that. Upon further inspection of this 1954 Chevrolet Bel Air, we found it to be fully loaded. Besides the really cool sun visor, this car had power windows, power seats, power brakes, dual 1 barrel carburetors, and a split Offenhauser manifold with dual exhaust.

Tom wanted me to check on the price, but I've always been realistic. I just said, "No, I can't afford that".

Tom boldly retorted, "How do you know, unless you ask?" and proceeded to go in to ask for the price. They told him $650.00 and he came back out to where I was and without flinching, told me $400. Wow! Suddenly, I was very excited. I thoroughly checked out the '54. There was no question in my mind. I wanted it. So, Tom went back in and started negotiating. He told them "My brother only has $400.00, but the battery is dead and we'll have to buy a new one, so we'll give you $375.00. To my surprise, they agreed and we had a deal.

On the way home from Chuck Olson, we stopped by Sears to buy a battery, thinking they would have the best batteries. I was $2.00 short and the guy wouldn't give me a break or let me come back. I then realized that I had a signed blank check from my mother on me to pay for my car insurance. I would give him mostly cash and pay off the balance with the check. I was then told they couldn't except 2nd party checks. So, off to Schucks I went and got my battery with no hassles. I held a grudge against Sears for a long time. I no longer do, but I rarely ever go into Sears thanks to one overzealous salesman.

As nice as it was for its years and miles, the BelAir was far from perfect and suffered from some deferred maintenance. I eventually needed a car to take me to a real job and back, so I parked the old '54 and bought something more reliable. The car sat for about 10 years before I paid it much attention again. The engine had seized and it had begun its journey on the road to old car heaven. In reality, it had a lot more problems than I realized when I purchased it, hence the low price tag. I bought another '54 the same color and figured that between the two, I could make one nice one.

I had also purchased a '65 Impala SS convertible that I (actually my brother) eventually fixed up to the point that it was not really an everyday car. So now, I had to buy another daily driver. My stable had grown to four cars, but I didn't want four cars. What I really wanted was a '54 Chevy convertible and a daily driver.

Low and behold, three weeks later as I was reading the classified ads in the Seattle Times, I saw a '54 Chevy convertible for $8300.00 and decided it might be time to implement a plan to get down to two cars, but that would involve owning five cars first. I told my brother Tom about my concerns and he casually countered, "Just go get it".

Grabbing my other younger brother, Bruce, my car guru, we headed out to take a look at what I hoped was a solid car. It was rough, but complete and best of all, there was no rust. The owner stated that it ran fine and I took his word for it. We made a deal and I put some cash down. I had probably offered him more than it was worth at the time. He took the down payment and agreed to hold it for a month until I could get the balance of the money together.

As the month went by, I raised the money and Bruce went with me to bring it home. The car was up on Whidbey Island, which was either a long drive or a ferryboat ride. We opted for the ferry and left the house at about sucks

o'clock in the morning and arrived around 7:30. Of course, we got there and the car didn't run.

The owner tells us that he has to go to work and heads out while Bruce and I stand by the car, wondering what we had gotten ourselves into. We borrowed a few tools that he made us promise to return. Now, we had to wait for the local automotive store to open at 9 am.

The car had a "mickey rigged" 12-volt battery in it, so we put an original 6-volt back in, and with some other tinkering by Bruce, the car was running again. I was afraid to shut it off, so we filled the gas tank with the engine running and took the long way home.

Now that it was home, it was time to get it titled and licensed. The car had been a California car, given to the old boy by his Godfather.

We had gotten it running well enough for a Washington State Patrol inspection, so off I went. When I arrived for the inspection, I was greeted by two men that didn't seem a day younger than 80. They did not appear to like their jobs and when they were finished, they handed me a piece of paper and simply said, "Here ya go!" They told me the car's VIN number didn't match the one on the title. I innocently asked, "Will I still be able to get it licensed?" They said, "I don't see how" and walked into their office.

Now I'm freaking out. I just paid good money for this car and I don't want to give it up. I decided to call the guy I bought it from and got no answer. I waited for what seemed like forever, which more than likely amounted to about 15 minutes. I called directory assistance, trying to find a number for the name that appeared on the title.

An elderly sounding man answered my call and I explained who I was and why I was calling. He screamed at me, "He sold it!"

I told him, "He said he needed money to buy a house."

"How much did you pay for it?" he asked.

"$8,000.00" was my reply.

"Ei-ei-ei-eight thousand?" he yelled.

After a moment of silence, he calmed down and we had

a pleasant conversation. I asked about the car's history and if he was the original owner. He said he wasn't, but that he had owned the car since 1956. He kindly offered to send me the original owner's manual and, good to his word, he did.

At this point, I was sure I had a clean car. I took it over to licensing and explained the situation. They asked if I had anything from the State Patrol. I showed her what I had and she simply asked if that actually was the correct number. I said "Yes." She asked if I wanted to license it today and I said "Yes." She then asked how much I paid for it and I told her. It looked like I was going to get a title and license, if I had enough money. So, I asked her approximately how much it would be. She told me and it looked like I would have about $3.00 left over.

She said, "Let's be sure" and added it up on the adding machine. As luck would have it, I had a nickel too much. I have always felt bad for not going back and giving her a dozen roses or something else to make her day. She surely made mine.

I guess you could say my brother changed my life on the day that he wheeled and dealed for my first '54. The new '54 has many of the parts from the first one on it. My

 favorite parts would be the power steering and the oil filter. Apparently, the oil filter was an option in 1954. My brother Tom owns a body shop in Seattle and he helped me with the resto-ration. I know I am biased, but I can honestly say I have never seen a nicer '54 Chev anywhere. Thanks, Tom!

Now days, I help put on some very successful charity driven car shows that raise money for those that need

a helping hand and in the back of my mind, I hope this serves as my dozen roses for my angel at the DMV. I should probably thank the old guy that owned the body shop that fired me, too, and maybe even the guy driving the Government Issue station wagon. Without them, I might never have found that first BelAir and wound up hooked on '54 Chevys!

I Needed a New Toy

by David Dickinson

I've always enjoyed buying and selling cars and somehow, in the last few years, my attention has been drawn to pickups. Not much into tearing huge swaths of vegetation from my yard and loading up to go to the dump, I can't site a particular need for a truck. We aren't planning on moving soon and I don't even buy them to use as daily drivers, but as toys to play with. Maybe I like to sit high in the saddle, so to speak, or maybe it's just the rugged feel of a Twin I-Beam suspension, but my last two acquisitions have been half ton pickups; '66 and '69 Fords to be specific.

For about ten years, starting in the mid '90s, I did drive a full size super cab 4X4 pickup as a daily driver. But, that was when gas was under $1.50 per gallon. I wouldn't want to feed that truck on a daily basis in today's economy. In reflection, I didn't need a truck then, either. Of course, there is a lot of security in having a full sized truck wrapped around you as you blaze down the highway amidst a myriad of poor drivers, all too wrapped up in cell phone calls, text messages, putting on makeup, eating Danish, shaving, drinking coffee, or putting final touches on the report that the boss was expecting on their desk last night. Does anyone just focus on driving anymore?

So, a few years ago I had found a buyer for a classic sports car that had been my toy for a while. I really enjoyed the car, but I had had it for too long in the overall scheme of things (my neighbors accuse me of changing cars like most people change underwear) and it was really a fair weather car that sat for most of the year. It was simply time to make a change; simply for the sake of change. I found a buyer down in Texas and the transport truck had no more than pulled away when I began to sweat, my palms starting to itch. A deep and gripping melancholy pervaded my very soul. There was an empty spot in my garage. I had to find a new toy.

The internet has completely replaced the newspaper for locating classic cars. So, I grabbed a cup of coffee and Danish, even though I wasn't hitting the highway, and went to my office to see what interested me. As a consultant to For Sale by Owners selling their classic cars, I counsel and encourage my clients to know the value of their vehicle to a potential buyer and to do everything they can to make their vehicle ready to get top dollar. As a buyer, I am looking for bargains; those gems that need a little shining up or where the sellers are uneducated when it comes to value. That doesn't make me unique; just smart.

Not having a particular vehicle in mind, I started searching by dollar range. I may not be rich, but I sure am cheap, so I started low. No sense in putting everything I had from the sports car into the next vehicle, right? That's exactly what I was thinking.

I have a pretty good knowledge base when it comes to value because of what I do, but I also rely on established pricing guides, as well. So, when I spot what I think might be a "score", I always double check myself. Once I find a handful of vehicles I think warrant further attention, I start making phone calls, asking very specific questions, trying to root out the truth and get past the advertised text. Sometimes, when an ad says "Like new paint" you have to ask "Which side?"

I found a 1966 Ford F100 Custom Cab with a 390cid V8 that had about 10,000 miles on the rebuild. It looked pretty

good for the price listed, but I noticed that it was out in the boondocks and quite a ways away from the general population. This guy was going to have a hard time getting any traffic to his home to actually see the truck. If it looked nearly as good as his pictures, it might be a good buy. Keep in mind; they hardly ever look as good up close as they do in pictures. I called him and asked him to send some more pictures.

In talking with him, he promised that the truck was all that he said it was, ran good, looked as good as the pictures, and I really should come out and take a look. He didn't sound desperate, but motivated.

I made an appointment and took the long journey to go meet him and see the truck, prepared to be disappointed, but curious just the same. It's a game that must be played in order to find the good bargains. While he said this truck didn't need anything, I thought his price was way too low for that to be reality. My job was to sort through the B.S. So, off I went.

I arrived at his home and he came out to greet me. We chatted a bit and he asked me to wait a moment, he'd be right back. I shuffled my feet in the driveway, wondering why he had me standing there when around the corner comes the prettiest green pickup I'd ever seen. Instantly, I was smitten. It really did look as good as the pictures on my computer. Maybe better. Mentally slapping myself across the face, I came back to my senses and started listening for sounds both good and bad. It had a nice exhaust note and no apparent body squeaks and rattles. He pulled to a stop and let it idle. It appeared to run smooth and quiet, except for the low and mellow tone emanating from the rear pipes.

Visually, I was in love. It looked great, but driving this beast was going to be a different story. Knowing before I ever left my house that it was a three speed on the column and had Armstrong steering and manual brakes, I came to look anyway. Hey, I'm a tough guy. I could handle it. Besides, I had a value size bottle of Aleve.

Looking at the 13" Grant steering wheel and clutch pedal, I began to wonder. Of course, "the proof is in the pudding" and so we jumped in and took off down the long

straight driveway. Upon coming to the street, I had to make a right turn and operate the foreign clutch. We were about to find out just how tough I was.

Firmly gripping the tiny steering wheel, I reefed as hard as I could, letting out the clutch and feathering the gas. It wasn't easy, but I made it around the corner and went through the gears. My old knee was going to get a workout if I drove this on a regular basis. In my mind, I questioned if I was up to doing this all the time. I would have preferred to have an automatic with power steering.

We drove a wide loop out in the country, which took us from his house around rural roads for about eight miles. This gave me a pretty good feel for the truck. I told the owner I wanted to run it up to 60-65 real quick just to see how it tracked, etc. Well, I went from 45 to 70 before I could get my foot off the gas pedal. Acceleration was no problem. It ran great, but the steering and clutch were both issues in my mind. Did I want to take it on? Could I get used to it? It sure was pretty.

In the end, I decided that I would let the money decide. I told you I was cheap! I came to look at it because the price seemed low and it was. Now then, if I could get him to come down a bit more, I might be able to justify my irrational actions. So, I made my offer. It was really low. This was where he started talking about why he was selling it. It seems that he bought it without his wife's blessing and it was becoming a "point of contention". While that may not be an issue in many homes, it was in his. He had paid more for it than he was asking and had recently done work to it. He was losing money already, he told me. I didn't respond. I just let him stew. In the end, he came back with a number that surprised and delighted me. We had a deal.

I drove the truck for only a few months in that summer of 2009, wrenching on the steering wheel and pushing the clutch, each time wondering whether I was having as much fun as I was telling myself I was having. I took it to car shows, cruises, and made the rounds to lots of gatherings. In the end, my sore arms and knee won out. I placed a compelling ad for the truck on Craigslist and a few other free advertising sites, stating that it was "fun to drive" and that the "great paint, custom interior, custom wheels, Grant steering wheel, AM/FM/Cass and tonneau cover turns Grandpa's truck into a modern work horse or weekend toy." Then, I waited for the calls and emails. It didn't take long before I found a buyer up in Canada. He came down with his son and drove it away. My arms and knee felt better already.

As always, I made a significant profit on the truck and gathered more fond memories. I had even built some muscle in my arms. Mostly, I had fun with the people involved in this old car hobby.

Some Things Just Go Together

by Dave Darby

Have you ever found yourself on an old two lane highway and looked down the road in wild wonder at the things you'd never see from the interstate? Barns, farmhouses, old motels, gas stations, tractors and more... Real Americana.

The old two lane highways evolved from Indian trails, to stagecoach lines, to dirt roads, and finally to highways. The paths they take are steeped in history, filled with the ghosts of millions of forgotten travelers. Towns, farms, and school houses were built alongside them as they meandered over hills and valleys, curving around, and dodging property lines.

I was lucky enough to grow up during the waning heyday of these times, when the two lane US highway was king and motels had names like the Crown, Archer, and A-Ford-O. It was a time when you could pull up to a gas pump and a uniformed attendant would fill your tank with hi-test, clean your windshield, and check your oil.

Some of these old motels and service stations survive to this day and all you have to do is get off the beaten track and go look for them. For instance, in Brooklyn, Iowa, on Old US 6, there is a Standard station that was built in the

1930's where you can still get full service. More than that, you can make new friends. People in these small towns have more time to stop and chat, swapping stories, and sharing history. Indeed, you come away from these places with far more than just your purchase. What a change from today's modern interstates that are built as straight and flat as possible with nothing older than an occasional McDonalds. There is no history or individuality on an in-terstate. What you find there is mass produced in the name of profit.

These old American highways are a great drive for any car, but they're even more perfect for your vintage car. After all, what other really cool ways do you have to enjoy a classic car? You can park them in your garage and stare at them, bring them to a car show and sit in a chair by them, or you can drive them ... but where? Certainly not on the interstate.

With the windows down (the perfect way to enjoy an old car), it's too noisy on the freeways, plus dodging the semi-trucks on a mega-multi-lane freeway bereft of scenery takes all of the joy away. But, that old two lane highway beckons you toward a relaxing tour of real Americana and becomes your own personal comfort zone. With the windows down, you can smell the wild flowers and occasional pig manure. It's all part of the experience, of course.

The best roads are those old stretches of pavement untouched by time, much like the car I am about to describe to you, which is perhaps the penultimate car to take on a road trip like this one.

Many street rods you find at your typical car show have been built within the past few years, with nary a vintage part on them. As you wander around through the mixture of fiberglass, billet, and steel, you may find yourself longing for that sense of history, that soul of a long forgotten mechanic twisting wrenches in the midnight oil back in the Eisenhower era. That smell of old mohair and naughahyde, decades old grease, oil, and rust is missing in today's street rods, many of which are basically just glorified kit cars. Even your restored cars have paint and finishing materials on them that was manufactured in the last two or three years.

But, Dave Southwick's '40 Ford coupe is different from these cars – completely different. There is not one piece on this car that is newer than 1957. In fact, the last time something was added to this car was in 1957. This ride is a genuine Hot Rod survivor. The real deal, with soul and genuine history. So let's set the "wayback machine" to 1950. Settle in and follow the story of Shorty's Ride.

Bill "Shorty" Etes bought this car in 1950 from the original owner, who purchased it new in 1940 from Williamson Ford in Rockford, Illinois. While we don't know his name, we do know that he took excellent care of the car in his 10 years of ownership. The paint, chrome, and interior are the same that Henry the first gave it way back in 1940.

Shorty and his brother Jim drove the '40 in stock form until 1953 when they were bitten by the need for speed. Forsaking Henry's flathead, they hustled on down to the local Cadillac dealership and hauled home a brand new 331cid V8 crate motor. They adapted the Caddy to a Lincoln overdrive tranny and two speed rear end. To provide some extra whoa to the go, Lincoln air cooled brakes were used at all four corners.

Over the next four years, Shorty and Jim constantly updated that Caddy engine with dual quads, a high lift cam, and lots of chrome. The car was well known as a street racer around the Etes' home town of Byron, Illinois, and

 showed its taillights to many an unsuspecting rod, as witnessed by a much younger Dave Southwick.

Unfortunately, tragedy struck in 1964 when Shorty passed away, a victim of sugar diabetes. The car was put into storage for the next twelve years. During this time, Shorty's brother Jim also passed on in 1971. Dave, having known the family for years, finally convinced Shorty's and Jim's mom to part with the car that had so enthralled him as a young pup since 1976.

Dave has continued to take the same tender loving care of this car as the previous owners and is justifiably proud of its hot rod heritage. Dave took me for a ride in this rod a while back and it was so much more than just a ride. There is something special about riding in an unrestored 74 year old hot rod. The sound, the smell, the feel, all take you back to a time long passed. Anyone who has ever ridden in an old unrestored car knows what I am talking about. Sure, the car has a few signs of wear. The paint on the tops of the fenders is getting thin and there are a few frays in the upholstery, but who cares when that's the same stuff that this car has worn since it left Dearborn all those years ago?

The materials and methods that make up this car are long ago forgotten and irreplaceable. Indeed, this car is a rarity. I took a whiff of that unmistakable aroma, a mixture of 70 plus year old mohair, rubber, oil, and gasoline. I listened to the exhaust that hasn't been emasculated by a catalytic converter and it took me back to my youth, when horsepower was king. This was a time when romance was found at the sock hop or the soda shop, not on a dating site, and when teenagers were wrenching on old iron instead of playing video games.

But, unlike a video game, this was a real time machine rolling me back to bygone days. Looking out through that two piece windshield over a pointed hood while driving down those same roads just like Shorty and Jim did, listening to the purr of that throaty Cadillac mill, was if those two were looking over our shoulders from the back seat and smiling in satisfaction of a job well done.

Dave Southwick is a keeper of history and is preserving the legacy that he has been entrusted with and for that, our hot rodding community owes him a debt of gratitude.

Mowing Lawns and Model Cars

by Steve Merryman

My daughter's boyfriend plays in a band called Letters from Traffic. The lead singer writes songs while he is stuck in traffic. I blame the recollection of this story on a traffic jam last night. I had lots of time to relive some of my youth sitting in that traffic and while I don't write songs, I love to write stories.

So, what formed you into the hot rodder you are? If you were Professor Peabody and had just upsized the Way Back Machine, what is the one car you'd bring back from the past for your very own? I got thinking about that and decided I could probably blame my interest in old cars on mowing yards and AMT model cars… among other things.

The first car I can vaguely recall my dad owning was a '36 or '37 Chev humpback, but the first one I truly remember well was a grayish blue '38 Chev business coupe. I recollect riding to kindergarten in it and climbing around on the back window shelf. Dad or mom's younger brother, who lived with us for a time, must have been into hot rodding a little bit, because I remember Little Books being in the house occasionally.

I attempted to paint my bicycle fenders in silver with some metallic green flames and tried the same thing on the lawn mower, too. That was probably around 1958 or so. I have no idea where I got the idea other than seeing it in a magazine, because I don't remember ever seeing a hot rod where we lived out by Sea-Tac Airport.

My first spark of really getting into cars was caused by a Christmas present when I was about 10 years old. It was a model of the Boyle Special Maserati, driven by Wilbur Shaw, that had won the Indy 500 in 1939. It was maroon plastic and had these neat water transfer decals. I think I was hooked right then and there. Mom thought any model car was fair game and I can remember her buying a succession of lame European model cars. One that really sticks in my brain was a Ford Cortina four door.

I'm surprised I didn't get into fighter airplanes, because they were way cooler than that damn little car. There was only one way I was going to be able to get the cars I wanted and that was to buy them with my own money, so I started mowing yards.

We had a State patrol trooper living next door named Sergeant Dick Crook. I swear to God, his last name was Crook. I think he paid me a dollar to mow his yard with his mower. Now, a dollar in those days would buy a loaf of bread, a quart of milk, and a pound of hamburger and still leave three cents for candy. After all, sales tax was only 2% and Bazooka bubble gum was a penny apiece.

There was a hobby shop out on Highway 99 called French's. Old man French was into model trains mostly, but he kept a shelf full of model cars for sale, too. I didn't spend the 25 cents I got for allowance each week. I saved every penny. Dad took me there after I had saved $3.00 or so. I don't really remember what car I bought the first time I went to the model shop, but there was a string of really cool cars that I decided were worth spending my hard earned money on.

We moved to our big house in 1960 and I started mowing the divorcee's yard a couple of lots down from us. She had a big damn yard with a cesspool in the back.

Geez, that thing stank, but she paid me a couple of bucks every time I mowed it.

She had a '55 Mercury with the glass roof and she drove me up Military Road one Saturday to a different model shop up on top of Reagan's Shell station. I don't know how she knew about my obsession, but maybe my folks told her. Thinking back now, if I'd been a couple of years older she would have seemed pretty hot.

She dropped me off and said she'd be back in a bit. The model shop (I have no idea what it was really called … it was always just referred to as the model shop) was maybe 300 square feet and stuffed with model boxes and all the necessary paraphernalia. AMT had just introduced the "Ala Kart" kit and that was my first purchase out of the small shop. The kit was a buck and a quarter, Testor's glue was 10 cents, and I think the Testor's paint kit that included silver among the seven little bottles was about 79 cents. Getting silver always seemed to be a big deal for some reason. Over the next few years, I think I bought and built the Ala Kart about three more times.

I was mowing her yard one particularly hot Saturday and the cesspool was really cooking. I was about ready to barf up breakfast when I spied something green. I picked it up and there was Abe with that little half smile looking back at me. I don't know the truth of whether it was a plant or truly a misplaced $5 bill, but my parents taught me that I shouldn't just pocket something without at least making an attempt to find the rightful owner. I debated with myself about what to do for the rest of the morning.

When I was done, I went up to the divorcee's door to tell her I was leaving and get paid. I remember thinking how hard honesty can be, but went ahead and told her about finding the money. She never batted an eye and told me she hadn't lost anything and that it was definitely mine. I think that was the first time I realized she was hot!

I vividly remember having seven bucks burning a hole in my pocket and the mile walk up the hill from our place to the model shop didn't take very damn long.

AMT had a kit called the Double Dragster. It was a two in one kit that had a streamlined, slingshot dragster and the wickedest Fiat altered you could possibly build. The kit came molded in bright red plastic and it was two dollars. I don't remember the other car I bought, but I'm sure with that much money I would have bought a second kit.

I got a reputation for doing a good job of mowing and a couple of other neighbors asked me to do their yards. Old man Rock across the street had me do his a couple of times. His yard must have been close to a half acre and he was a tight-fisted old goat. I think he only paid me a dollar or so, but he had the neatest pile of crap out back, including a post war, pale blue Packard sedan. He told me that if I'd save enough money, he'd sell it to me. I don't know how long it sat there, but it was still back there when I moved away several years later.

There was a family down at the end of the street that was kind of a wild bunch. Mostly, they were into motorcycles, but there were a few cars, too. I was mowing their yard one morning when I spied a somewhat oxidized dark blue '53 Ford hardtop. It had Lakes Pipes, flipper hub caps, and white tuck and roll interior. In script, painted on each "B" pillar, was "Mood Indigo". I assume it was named for the old Duke Ellington song. It may have had spotlights, too, but my memory is getting a little short on details. I couldn't remember ever seeing the car on the street, but the whole package made a really lasting impression. I think that was the first custom car I had ever seen.

The Olsen brothers next door and I got into drag racing our model cars. If we had been smart, we'd have copyrighted the idea because we were at least a couple of years ahead of Hot Wheels. If you built models in the early 1960's, you'll remember the solid metal axles, front and rear, that passed through plastic blocks glued to the frame. The wheels pressed onto the metal axles, which were usually splined into the wheels, and you could lower the car from stock by inverting the plastic blocks. This was a pretty slick system for rolling fairly easily and going in a straight line and isn't that what drag racing is all about?

We had a piece of Formica about 10 feet long that had come out of their kitchen remodel. We discovered that gutting the cars and putting dad's wheel weights inside made them go faster. We also discovered that pouring a little Testor's glue on the hood and lighting it with a match made things even more interesting.

It wasn't too long after this that I started driving for real and working at the Standard station across the street from the model shop. One day, I came to work and the model shop was nothing more than a pile of wood debris and a sign proclaimed it to be the site of a new Safeway.

Reagan's moved over to the other corner but didn't include a new model shop and the little grocery store behind our gas station went out of business shortly after the Safeway opened.

I drive up that way every once in a while. The old neighborhood hasn't changed a great deal. It's just a little more time worn. I find myself thinking back to that magic four or five years and then get on eBay looking for AMT models. You can still find the Ala Kart and the Double Dragster, but they appear to be reissues. Somehow, a reissue just will never quite recapture the original.

I Couldn't Catch a Break

by David Dickinson

In 1957, after wrecking his '49 Chevrolet, my step dad bought a slightly used '56 Chevrolet 210 two door sedan. Not a person to feel a great need for a lot of power or convenience items like an automatic transmission, power steering or brakes, he picked out a no frills six cylinder, three speed model.

My first real memory of the car was one night when we were visiting family friends and as we left to go home my fingers got shut in the door. It was a long time ago and I was pretty young, but I can vividly remember that night and how much it hurt. Luckily, my fingers were very small and nothing was permanently damaged, but it scared me enough to make sure it never happened again.

It was the family car for a few years, but in the major scheme of things, we didn't really go a lot of places as a family and the '56 usually wound up pretty dirty because it was dad's work car, as well. Being in construction and working with concrete, the car was always filthy by the end of the week; especially the back seat where he would throw his rain gear, dirty jackets, and the like. In fact, because he never really cleaned the car, it was always a grimy mess.

Growing up, I was always aware of car designs and I remember how each year the car dealerships would paper the huge showroom windows and hide the new models until the official release date. As we all know, the '56 Chevrolets were an instant and timeless classic and from the time that my generation was old enough to drive and start buying cars, it was "the one to have", along with the two years before and after. I say this because, as I grew older and began dreaming of the day I would start driving, I was glad we had the '56 and I was certain that it was just waiting for my turn to get behind its wheel.

When that time came, my parents had bought a brand new '66 Chevrolet station wagon as the "family car" and like the '56, it had no frills. It was a Biscayne with a six cylinder three speed and it didn't even have a radio. My mother was the one that I got to practice driving with mostly and so, it was the wagon that I drove most. That was OK, but I couldn't wait to get the '56 out on the road on my own.

For some reason, when it came time to take my driving test, it was decided that it would be in the '56. As a result

of very little time behind its wheel, I flunked the driving test. Oh, I did just fine out on the streets; signaling properly, stopping when required and doing all the right things I needed to do to satisfy the clip board toting test official. However, when we pulled back into the DMV station, the guy with the clip board instructed me to pull up to a set of cones in a side parking area. He wanted me to park between them! I failed miserably.

I had only parked the Driver's Ed car during after school classes and that was in a new mid-size model with power steering and a much tighter turning radius. I would have to return two weeks later to try again. That meant

92

two more weeks without a license. I was not a proud and happy camper and my love of the '56 turned to disdain for a brief moment in time.

I was allowed to practice parking the '56 a few times before the test. After I managed to successfully park it between the cones for the guy with the clip board, I was rewarded with the little wallet sized piece of paper that all teenagers coveted.

Now began the process of devising a plan and excuse to "borrow the car". It took a few weeks of asking and being rejected, but finally, the old man relented and said yes. There was a dance at a church a few miles from the house and I was to go there and come right home. Sure! That's what I was going to do. I wasn't really interested in going cruising or showing off. I just wanted to go to the dance. Uh huh ... sure!

Well, I finally had keys in hand and off I went. I did go to the dance; several times, in fact. I went in and wandered around, talked to friends, danced a little and tried to be good, but before long I could hear the car calling to me. "Come on", it would say. "No one will know!" I relented to its badgering and headed out the door the first time and drove around for a short time, but figured I'd better go back where I was supposed to be.

After hanging out at the church dance for a while, I heard the car calling again and off I went. I was a little more confident now and so I put it through its paces. I had never had an opportunity to "put my foot into it", so to speak, so I gave it a try. The 235ci six cylinder motor was pretty strong for its time and I discovered that I could grab a pretty mean second gear. I'd wind it up in first until I was ready to shift and then executed the clutch and column shifter with lightning speed. I had never seen anyone shift that fast and was told by a buddy that it was the fastest he'd ever seen, as well. My confidence soared. These short excursions continued throughout the evening.

I was to be home no later than 11 o'clock and so, I pulled up and walked into the house at about ten minutes before. Dad had gone to bed and Mom was there waiting up to make sure I got home safe, like she always did. I told her I'd had a fun time at the dance and went to my room to recount my adventures on the road.

To this day, I have no idea how he knew what the mileage on the odometer was before I left, but the next day the old man wanted to know how I had put 36 miles on the car going to the church and back. I was speechless. I wasn't keeping track of miles and had no idea whether he had snuck out and looked before I left or if he was just assuming that I had violated his trust or if he was just fishing to see my reaction. In any event, it was a while before I was allowed to use the car again.

Before the next time out in the car, I had figured out how to disconnect the speedometer cable after putting on an appropriate number of miles. I figured that should grant me immunity from getting caught going farther than my agreed journey. So I thought.

The next time I used the car, I was all over town and had a great time cruisin' 6th Ave, a magical stretch of asphalt where all cars cool and not so cool, filled with teens and young adults, gathered in various locations for either slow cruises or brief races between red lights. I had a blast!

Again, I was busted the following morning. He wanted to know why a friend of his would ask what his car had been doing all the way up in the north end of town late on a Saturday night. I had no response and wasn't courageous enough to challenge him with a simple "What? You think that's the only blue and white Chevrolet in town?" I had to face the music and the fact that it would be a long time before he was going to throw me the keys again.

Keep in mind, each time I wanted to borrow that car, I had to clean it or be embarrassed by its considerably less than stellar condition. Even back then, I was no slouch when it came to detailing a car. I washed, vacuumed, waxed, and polished it to the best of my ability with the time I had between gaining approval and departure time.

One of the last times I borrowed the '56 was to go to another dance. My brother and a couple of our friends were along this time and while I wanted to be good, I caved to peer pressure. We went cruisin' and raisin' hell in general. One of the guys was really good at "flipping" bottle caps between his thumb and finger and he had a propensity to pick them up wherever he went. That night he had a pocket full and he was flipping them out the windows and around the inside of the car. I didn't think much of it until the next morning when the old man wanted to know why there were beer caps littering the back floor of his car. I couldn't catch a break.

It wasn't long after the "beer cap" episode that I finally bought my first car. Ironically, I found a '56 Chevrolet that I paid $150 for and not only was it a Bel Air, but it had a V8 and an automatic transmission. He never said so, but I'm sure that didn't please my step-dad. It was a pretty nice car for the money and only needed brakes before I could insure and drive it... wherever I wanted to. That was the beginning of a string of old cars that I bought and sold in high school.

As time went by and Dad was getting close to retiring, I told him that I would like to have his '56 when he was done with it and ready to buy a new car. As fate would have it, that time came when I was off traveling the world in the Navy and my brother was back home from the Marines. He did give me the car and I was grateful. I just wasn't there to enjoy it. Not long after that, my parents  decided to sell the family home that my brother and I had grown up in and so, my brother bought it to raise his new family. Because I was gone and not planning on being back soon, I decided to pass the car on to my brother and sister-in-law.

He has raised his daughters and they are off on their own, but he still has the car and it "lives" in the same garage as it has since 1957 when our parents first brought it home.

The car has been repainted once and the original front seat replaced because the frame cracked, but it has been in a dormant state for over twenty years. Amazingly, it still has less than 100,000 miles. At this point, my brother and sister-in-law are digging in and doing the basics to get it back on the road. While there had been visions of modernizing the running gear with a small block V8 and automatic transmission, they have decided to simply get it running again and leave it stock. Whatever they decide is great. I'm just happy that it's still in the family.

Therapeutic Goat

by Bobby Eidem

Ihave a car for sale. I've only had it a handful of months. It's a '66 Pontiac GTO that I bought on a whim to help a friend of my nephew. He's 35 years old, got a girl pregnant, and they're going to get married. This guy had owned "the Goat" for about five or six years and didn't want to part with it, but he needed the money. My nephew told him that I'm into old cars and so, they brought it over. I had an extra space in the garage and negotiated a more than fair price with him.

The expectant mother's family owned a mechanic shop over in Torrance. He gave me all the paperwork on the car that he had generated and the file from the previous owners. There is a lot that is right with the car and he's spent over $13,000 on it through the family business. It's a great car and I've been straightening out some small issues that they hadn't gotten to. Someone put a radiator and fan setup in and it kept blowing fuses. After looking at it closer, I determined that each fan needed its own fuse; its own hot line. Somebody had both fans connected to one fuse. I've finished the last of those minor issues and I've got it all straightened out now. I wanted it to be problem free when I passed it on.

I got the car for a reasonable sum and figured I'd fix it up a little bit, turn it, and make a couple grand. So, I stripped the motor down, took the TriPower off, repainted the block, cleaned it up a bit, and put it all back together just the way it's supposed to be.

I have it for sale for $35,000. It books out at $38,000 with the four speed, but it's not matching numbers. It has a 400cid in it. If it had the numbers matching 389cid, it would up it another twenty-five percent. Like every other car for sale, it will sell when the right guy comes along. I'm in no hurry. I do this sort of stuff for therapy.

I received a phone call about "the goat" from a woman one day. She explained that she wasn't calling to ask the typical questions a car buyer might ask, saying that she wanted to know if she could rent my car for a few hours. She went on to explain her odd request. Her husband, Gordon, had a GTO 4-speed, similar to the one I was selling when he was younger.

Gordon had come down with cancer and the doctors were going to begin chemo and radiation treatments. Because the outcome was uncertain and cancer treatment has a way of really taking its own toll she asked if there was some way possible, before he started his chemo, that she could rent the car for a few hours to let him play with it.

When I heard his story it touched my heart, because we're all getting older, all of us car guys. I started to feel my own mortality, thinking he's even younger than I am. He's 65 and I'm 70. So, I told her there wouldn't be a problem. Considering the circumstances, I wouldn't rent it to her, but all I really would want is some identification and insurance information.

We set up an appointment for them to come over and she asked me to have the car in the driveway. So, when they drove up she told Gordon, "I have a surprise for you" and there was my GTO sitting in the driveway. I was watching them from inside the house. They walked up to the car and he was looking all around it. I could see the stars in his eyes. Then they both started to walk to the front door and I greeted them at the bottom of the staircase. I thought I saw stars in his eyes, but they were actually tears. So then, she explained to him that I was letting them take the car for a few hours to go play with it. He was almost balling and I was choking back my own tears. It was really an amazing moment.

He said that he had owned a black one and had to drive it at night, because his also didn't have air conditioning, nor did it have power steering or power brakes. When he'd go for any real distance, he said he would always drive at night, going from point A to point B, because it was so damned hot in the car. We just kind of laughed about that. My car has a Hurst shifter from the factory, so it has no power accessories or air conditioning, either. It's basically like his was, but it's blue and his was black. They do get hot inside. Another difference is that he bought the black car brand new. I don't know how long he had the car, but apparently, it was stolen. So, he obviously had great admiration for the GTO. It had been his favorite car.

To start out, I took them for a ride in it. It's a four speed with 3.55 gears and tri-power. It really launches, so I drove the car and got on it a little bit and then put him behind the wheel to drive back. I coached him and nudged him, saying "Go ahead and step on it. You know, kick in those other two carburetors. Feel the GTO."

His car also had tri-power. So he got on it, and as we were driving back into my neighborhood, I said, "Look, I want you to drive it like you stole it." Then I tapped him on the shoulder and said, "Don't steal it, though, okay?" We had another good laugh over that. When we pulled back in the driveway I said, "Go enjoy it and drive it like a GTO." I got out of the car and they left.

They were gone for about two hours and I got a phone call from Gordon's wife, Malka. She told me that they were down at the beach. I lived in Fullerton, about 30 miles away. They went to lunch and she told me that they might be a little longer than planned. I told her it wasn't a problem and that my only request was that they fill the gas tank before they brought it back.

When I asked, "How does Gordon like it?" she said, "Boy he's having a great time." So, I asked if he had scared her at all and she chuckled, saying he had a little and I joked, "Good, that's what it's all about, you know."

They brought the car back four hours later and I met them in the driveway. We talked about where they went and about his experience driving the "Goat." I took a picture of them with the car and they thanked me.

Malka gave me a copy of his medical report, which my wife and I read. It's pretty touching. The plan was to do a  bone marrow transplant and start some chemo on his neck. That's where I guess all the cancer is located. So, you know, things don't look too good for him in the future.

I was just happy to do this for them. Without thinking about what might happen, I posted a comment about their visit and letting them take the car on Facebook and my daughter responded with a big posting saying I had done a "make a wish foundation" type of thing and everybody made a big deal about what a great guy her dad is. All the accolades I was getting kind of threw me. I wasn't expecting all the attention.

I just wanted to do something for the guy and his wife. It was an opportunity to make a difference in someone else's life and he had a great time. I was able to make him happy for a few hours and I just think that's something that us older car guys try to do when we can. I didn't expect anything from it and I'm sure most of my old car buddies would do the same thing.

In my opinion, the guy's wife really deserves the credit, because she found me and set it all up. So, I think that it's a great thing that she did for her husband and to me, she is the real hero of the story.

An Unexpected Swap

by David Dickinson

During the summer of 1969, between my junior and senior year in high school, I gained my personal freedom and immediately went out and started exercising it. I found freedom in the sense that my brother, a year older, had just graduated from high school, joined the Marines, and left for boot camp. In our house, it was no longer "the boys" … it was just me.

I had always been responsible enough and so, all of a sudden, watchful eyes had retired from service. My parents no longer were keeping close track of me and I came and went as I pleased without 20 questions or later reports of what I had been up to and with whom.

This was a particularly useful new family dynamic for me, considering my somewhat independent streak. I had time, money, and a car. Some of the time was spent working and the rest was spent playing with cars.

I had had numerous cars throughout high school and at this time I had what was probably the weirdest of any of them. It was a 1963 Chevrolet Biscayne four door sedan that was absolutely plain Jane looking from 10 feet or 100 feet. The exterior and interior color scheme by Chevrolet, with black rubber matting on the floor from the factory, dressed it down completely. It was nearly invisible on the street. It was, however, in mint condition inside and out.

How did I wind up with such a car? Well, I hadn't sought it out. I got it in a trade for a '56 Chevy 210 two door sedan that was as straight as a washboard, painted with a spray can, and had a 283cid that had been re-bored to 301cid many miles prior to my acquisition. It was looser than a goose and I knew it was not long for the world.

The trade went something like this...

I was out washing the '56 one day and a guy pulls up and gets out of his car and waves to me. I waved back, trying to figure out who it could possibly be. He didn't look familiar, but I hear him holler across the street "Hey Dave, how's it going?" Now I'm really at a loss.

As he proceeds in my direction, I put down the hose and wipe off my hands. He offers his and says, "You don't recognize me, do you?" I shake his hand and admit I am stumped. He says "I'm David Chamberlain. I used to live across the street!" I about fell over. His family had been there up until his father, a young man really, died of a heart attack one night. They had moved shortly after and I hadn't seen him since.

With that, I did recognize him and we chatted amiably for a while when he popped the question he had been chomping at the bit to ask. "Is your Chevy for sale?" I thought about it for a moment and replied "I hadn't thought about it." Hell yes, I'd sell the car. It was about to come unwound.

"Actually, I hoped we could trade cars," he said. I have this '63 Chev I got from my grandfather and I'd rather have your '56. I drive by here all the time and think about stopping and seeing if it's still you guys that live here."

While I wasn't excited about a four door car any more than any self-respecting high school senior, I was excited about the possibility of having a car that would continue to run. This was a nice car even with the two extra doors and the plain Jane colors of Saddle Tan outside and Medium Fawn inside to match the unexciting Biscayne model.

Bonus time came when he started to tell me about the car. His grandfather had ordered it new with the 300HP 327 V8, which came with a four barrel carb and dual exhaust. He had also ordered it with the posi rear end. It might be a bit of a sleeper when it came to the performance aspect!

"How's it run and drive?" I ask him.

"Well, it runs good, drives good and all that, but the valve guides are shot and the heads need to be done" he responded.

"Mine could use a few things, too", I reply simply and without a ton of detail. He goes on to tell me that he has an engine he wants to put in the '56 if I could see my way to trading him. I tell him that my engine needs to be re-placed anyway and if his car runs as good as it looks then I'd trade him.

The '63 did run as good as it looked and did, in fact, smoke a bit. No problem. I could swap out heads. We made our trade and off he went in the battered old '56 Chev, pouring the coals to the worn out old engine as he went down the street. To this day, I don't really know why he was so enamored with that particular '56 and I never did see him again and find out what he actually did with it.

Here is where it gets interesting.

After thoroughly detailing the Biscayne and making it as nice as it could be, I drove it for a few weeks. I had rounded up some nice beauty rings and Red Line Wide Oval tires to put on it and they looked pretty nice with the stock hubcaps. I decided that I just couldn't live with the puffs of smoke coming out of the back and opted to have the heads rebuilt. I took the risk that the bottom end would hold up and in the end, it did.

After taking the heads to the local machine shop, I cleaned everything up in preparation for putting it all back together. The engine compartment was pretty nice and dressed up well. I repainted the air cleaner and valve covers in the correct colors and awaited the heads.

A couple of days later and my buddy, Craig, and I were turning wrenches and putting the rebuilt heads in place. Reassembly was completed and that old 327 V8 fired right up. New plugs, wires, points, and condenser were installed already and it was ready to be tweaked on the local gas station's scope. We had a friend who worked nights and access to the state of the art equipment. A little adjusting of the carb and timing really smoothed things out and there was absolutely no hesitation or vibration from the motor. It ran like new.

The first time down the street out of the shop convinced me that I had done the right thing by rebuilding the heads. Performance was increased and it ran like a raped ape, so to speak. The Powerglide worked well and the posi rear end hooked up and off it went.

A quick trip home to change clothes and I was back at Craig's house to pick him up. We proceeded with great haste to the local cruise spot in search of burgers, girls, and friends in cars. Finding all, we decided life was good.

One of the guys we ran into was Craig's neighbor, Tom. He owned a '63 Corvette split window. It was Silver Blue and had a 327 V8 with a four speed. It was a very nice car and was Tom's baby. Along with Tom was another young car guy, Fred.

Fred was a great guy, but pretty excitable and always ready to tease people to get a reaction. He had a gorgeous old Mercury coupe that he'd inherited from his father. I felt pretty out of place around these guys in my four door Biscayne and they threw their fair share of barbs my way, trying to get my goat.

Not one to buckle easily, I stepped out from around the back of my old lady ride and pulled Tom aside. I told him

I wouldn't expect to beat him so he didn't need to worry about losing face, but I had just done a tune up and was curious how my "door factory" would do in a side by side race from a rolling start.

We laughed together while imagining the sight of such a contest and agreed to a 40 mph rolling start. Once we were side by side, I would honk my horn and simply kick my Powerglide down to the only other gear it had available. Tom would do whatever he chose to in his four speed Corvette.

Fred jumped in with Tom and Craig was with me as we pulled out of the McDonalds where we had gathered. We were heading south on Pacific Ave. from 72nd St. as we pulled alongside of each other. Just as if the race gods had planned it all ahead of time, there was no traffic in front of us.

We hit 40 mph and I laid on my horn with my left hand and mashed the gas pedal with my right foot. The Biscayne squatted ever so slightly in the rear and barked off a light chirp of tires as we surged forward. On my right sat the Corvette, as if sitting still. As we continued to thrust forward, I stayed right next to the more performance oriented sport coupe. I was absolutely amazed.

Amazement gave way to reality as we hit about 100 mph and Tom pulled his shifter into 4th gear, finally pulling away. I immediately shut it down and turned around, heading back to McD's at a grandmotherly 32 mph. Once there, I parked and walked away from the car, leaving it as if it had been sitting there for an hour. I wanted to distance myself from the car in the event the cops had followed us.

My disassociation with my car lasted only a moment as the Corvette pulled in beside me with Fred jumping out, yelling "OK, what did you do to it?" I explained that I had rebuilt the heads and tuned it up. That was all.

"Start it up!" demanded Fred. I reached in through the window and tapped the key. The small block roared to life and purred like a kitten. "Pop the hood!" Fred further insisted. I walked around the front and casually lifted the hood. It was absolutely sweet; fresh and clean, running like a watch, with not a squeak, click, tap or hesitation. You could put your hand on the air filter and not feel the engine run. Fred was impressed. Tom ... well, not so much. Of course, he'd just had to struggle to best a four door Biscayne.

I had enjoyed the moment and felt blessed that I hadn't been pulled over by the police, who could probably care less how good my old car ran. I'd have lost my license for sure. Not that it would have been the first time. But, that's another story.

Model A Restoration 101

by Lenora Andres
For Tom Andres, Proud Owner and Car Nut!

My husband Tom bought his 1930 Model A Town Sedan in the summer of 1965, soon after completing his sophomore year at Central Washington State College. He needed a car to get to his summer job at St. Regis, as well as getting back and forth to college.

At work, he had become friends with Stan Irwin who told him about the "extra" Model A Town Sedan that he and his friend owned. They offered the car to him for $200. It was in very good original condition, needing only to replace a cracked oil ring in one of the cylinders. Tom's very first car was a Model A that he had purchased in 1962, so he had quite a bit of experience with them. Fixing the cracked oil ring was a piece of cake.

We met in 1968 when he caught my eye while driving his red '66 Chevelle 396 Super Sport. After we were engaged, he proudly showed me his "other" car, the Model A. I immediately fell in love with it and asked him if we could have it as our "get-away car" from the church instead of the Chevelle, but he said it wasn't fast enough!

We lived in apartments the first four years we were married, as Tom was going to graduate school in Ellensburg and we were saving up for our first home, which we purchased in 1971. The first item that went into our Fircrest home was that Model A! Tom couldn't wait to get started restoring it. In all appearances, it looked pretty good, but by that time, it was 41 years old and a bit worn all over, showing its "mid-life crisis"!

The task of restoring an old car like a Model A in a one-car garage isn't easy, but that was all we had and we were proud of it. We needed to take the body off the frame in order to restore the frame, as well as replace a lot of the oak in the body, which included the 2-inch thick body rails, all of the top roof bows, door framing, and connecting pieces.

We had just restored and polished the stainless steel radiator shell when Tom asked me if he could store it safely in one of our spare bedrooms. We had three bedrooms and no children at the time, so, I said, "Yes, of course!"

As the evening progressed and I was well into one of my favorite television shows, I was aware that Tom had been in and out of the house a lot. So, I got up to investigate. I discovered that he also brought in many of the other Model A parts, like the hood, in four large pieces, four doors, four fenders, the running boards, the headlights and light bar, the "ahooga" horn, the steering wheel, and steering column. The front and back seats had to be taken out and stored somewhere, so they came in, as well!

Model A aficionados know how much room just one fender takes up, but for those who don't, just know that the front ones alone, including the running board, are probably about the same length as a single bed.

One night, my parents dropped in for a visit and my mother, anxiously hoping for a grandchild in the near future since we had our home now, asked where a baby would be able to sleep with all those car parts in the bed-rooms. My resourceful husband just looked at her and said, "Well Elfrida, we would just take one of these nice curved front fenders, suspend it upside down from the ceiling and it would make a lovely cradle." My mother believed him!

Many hours were spent removing rusty bolts of all sizes before the body could be lifted off the chassis. The car then needed to be pushed half way out of the garage. We had a couple of good friends help us lift the body and set it sideways on saw horses inside the garage. In order to pull the engine out, my husband's resourceful thinking came up with the idea to use a large oak wood board connected between our camper jacks to use as an engine hoist. That was an unusual site, but we were always keeping the neigh-bors entertained!

Once the engine was removed, the frame could be pushed back into the garage to fit snugly up against the Model A body. The only way anyone was able to get through the garage, was by stepping carefully through the body. Wheels were then removed for restoration and the frame was held up with jack stands. The wood restoration was interesting in itself, as one needed to take very careful measurements and in some cases, make templates to use to cut the wood pieces out. All of the wood used in the Model A was oak, so it was very strong and quite heavy as well. Restoring the oak roof bows meant that first the oak was cut to the correct measurement, then they needed to be steamed and bowed, using vices to slowly bend them.

This process took place in our one bathroom tub, using steam from the teakettle. I cannot recall how many times we took turns refilling that tea kettle and heating it to boil-ing, but I know that we went through three tea kettles, as the bottoms would burn out if they got forgotten on the burner! Luckily, Sears kept us well stocked in tools and tea kettles.

The engine was rebuilt, covered, and stored in one corner of the garage. The wheels were sandblasted and stacked up in another corner of the garage. We carefully removed all of the paint from the whole body, doors, fenders, hood pieces, etc., often using sawhorses in the front driveway to hold the door or fender we were working on at the time.

With very little front driveway space that was level before it sloped down to the street, the back patio was also put to good use. We used body putty in little dents and crevices as needed. We sanded all of it many times and each time the sand paper we were using got finer and finer. This was my "Restoration Model A 101 class" taught by my husband Tom.

I fit right in with all of the car guys. Finger nails? None! I was proud of my worn down nails! Birthday and Christmas presents were often comprised of things like a Model A Ford Restoration books or a new radiator cap.

We made another trip to Sears for a compressor, spray gun, masks, and tons of masking tape. The restoration book was able to tell us the original colors for 1930 by looking up the serial number. It's another lesson to watch the paint being custom mixed. I had no idea the color red was used in the dark blue paint. At the time we restored the car, acrylic lacquer was easily obtainable. Many coats later, finely sanding in between coats, we had ourselves a beautifully restored Model A. Well, almost!

This process took the four full years while we lived in this particular home, but the top trim and getting the cloth interior and seats upholstered wasn't done until a few years later, after we moved into our next home in Lakewood. It wasn't long after that we found ourselves expecting our first child, so car restoration projects were on hold.

The car was a wonderful driver, and we had a lot of fun running around town. It always brought a smile to the  faces of people who remembered driving these cars in their youth and we thought of the car like a favorite grandfather! One of my most memorable times riding in the Model A was when I was pregnant and the baby was overdue, so my husband took me on a bumpy ride through the town of Steilacoom, hoping to speed things up.

We were finally able to have the upholstery done in 1980. The interior of the Model A was mostly mohair and quite expensive, but we decided it was worth it, so we made the commitment to go for it! It was quite a task to find a qualified upholster to do the job right, but the person we hired had excellent qualifications. He had been the chief upholsterer for the presidential jets at Andrews AFB and he did a beautiful job.

The Model A has provided many hours of fun with family and friends. After our two girls were grown, we joined the Tacoma Gallopin' Gertie's Model A Club, which has provided many opportunities to enjoy our car and share stories with other Model A fans.

When my husband was teaching school, he would often bring his Model A to give his 4th graders a ride on the school grounds at the end of the school year. One evening about five years ago, one of his former students called him to request not only his presence at her wedding, but asked if he would bring his Model A to be used as their "Get Away Car" from the church.

Tom has owned dozens of classic cars and enjoyed them all, but a guy's first cars are always special. Every time he drives the "A", he takes a trip down memory lane. We often hear people at car shows telling stories about the cars they have owned and wished they had kept one special car. For Tom,  that special car is still parked in our garage and is available to be driven and enjoyed. It has become a member of our family.

The Bug and the Girl

by David Dickinson

We all have different priorities in life, but as a young man in the US Navy it always amazed me that many, if not most, of my peers did not have cars. From my early years in high school and as soon as I was finished with my basic training and my first ship had settled into port, it was important to me to get a set of wheels.

My first foray into the affordable car market as a young sailor was a 1960 Corvair, which I soon traded for a 1959 Chevrolet Impala 2 door Sport Coupe. The Corvair was fun and the Impala was quite a score as trades go, and one of those cars I wish that I still had to this day, but that is not the subject of this story. The Impala had to be sold when my ship left port for a "WestPac" tour of duty, but upon return, I immediately found new wheels.

I had saved quite a bit of money while overseas and decided I wanted something newer to drive so, in 1971 I bought a '70 Fiat 850 Racer. It was just like an 850 Spider, a fairly small car, but it had a hardtop instead of a convertible top. I quickly realized that the Fiat was an oil leaker and that all of them were. I didn't get a bad car in particular. I got a bad car in general. I have always detested cars that leak and consider those that do of low character. If a car can't hold its oil, I don't have much use for it. This is an attitude that I developed after having a car in high school that required filling the oil and checking the gas daily.

Having displeasure with the Fiat, I returned to the dealer that had told me what a wonderful car it was going to be. I felt I needed to let him know that I thought his judgment was lacking, but was willing to give him one more chance if he would take the Fiat off of my hands and put me into something of equal value to what I had paid for it. I was young and naïve and unaware of the mathematical juggling acts practiced under the three ring circuses of auto dealerships in the early 1970's but, I drove away in a '69 Volkswagen Beetle … and that is the real subject of this story; my beloved Bug.

Oh, the adventures, the road trips, the nights out, and the economy. It cruised the highways and byways of southern California and up and down the entire West Coast many times. It was a discrete car for those indiscreet attacks on the evening and I could gas it up with my pocket change and run for days. There was actually money left to buy beer after I left the gas station! This was a car that was made for me. I could do mechanical surgery on it without hesitation and keep it in tune just like an old Chevy.

I had a close friend who had a '70 Bug and we would work on our cars together. Having our act down pat, almost any issue was simple. As an example, we could pull an engine, change a clutch, reinstall the engine and be driving down the street in less than an hour. I know this to be true, because we timed the process once.

There was a time when I thought I would have to part with the Bug. I had brought it up to Washington for about a year and a half, while my ship was in a yard period in Bremerton. This was a great time in my life because I was hanging with old friends and living near family. I also had a chance to see that the local job market was not good if I  were to get out of the Navy and expect to go to work. As a result of that valuable insight, I reenlisted and was assigned to instructor duty in San Diego.

I planned to take my '60 Austin Healy to California with me when I moved down there and the Bug was not going to fit into the plan. It was time to part with my beloved Beetle. I was pretty concerned with where it wound up and wanted to find a good home with an owner that would appreciate her the way I did. This was just like I might deal with a pet that couldn't move into an apartment. My, how we get attached to our cars!

So, I put the word out and it wasn't long before a pretty young lady I knew stepped up to claim ownership. There was a hitch, however. If she was going to buy the car, I had to promise to teach her how to drive a stick shift transmission. To be honest, I thought that was a pretty fair proposition. She was easy on the eyes, intelligent when it came to conversation and well, she was going to pay me my asking price. I just had to teach her how to walk the dog, so to speak.

Wanting to be sure my young trainee learned the proper way to drive my treasured Bug, we spent many hours together cruizin'. We had a lot of fun and really enjoyed each other's company. I was going to miss the car and I was getting to the point where I thought I might miss our lessons, as well.

I have to admit that the Bug was not without fault. By this time, it was over six years old and had a little slop in  the shifter, as some of the older VWs did. I was always very careful when shifting it and had a deft feel for a precise shift. My pretty young student lacked the same skillful touch and one sunny afternoon as we were "practicing" driving skills, a shift to second gear resulted in a sudden grinding of metal as the car was unceremoniously jammed into reverse, re sulting in an equally sudden halt of forward progress. My Bug had bit the proverbial dust.

My pretty young driving apprentice's eyes went wide with shock, disbelief, and fear. Mine closed as my head bowed and fell into my hands. I couldn't cry. I couldn't yell. I took a deep breath and lifted my head to the world ahead of me. In a flash, I knew what I would do. I would fix the car and keep it. It was the strangest impulse. I wasn't sure why, but I knew I should just keep the car.

To this day, I can't tell you where the notion came from but, I announced to my buyer that I was not going to sell the car and if she wanted to drive it she would just have to come down to San Diego. Did she want to move to San Diego with me? Well, guess what? She did. Her name was Denise and she became my wife. So, I kept the Bug and got the girl, too.

Alfa R. Veloce (1958-)

by Steve Walker

I always liked open wheel race cars of the '50s, like the midgets, sprints, and Indy cars. Side cars have always amused me with the auxiliary seating patched onto an otherwise symmetrical design. Why not combine them? A fine idea. Now what did I have to work with?

I had an Alfa Romeo that I had purchased on October 1, 1971 from A & B motors in the University District for $947. This was at the beginning my senior year at the University of Washington. It was a cute gray sports car with a difficult to open rag top. Larry Smith, who wrote a comic strip I illustrated for National Lampoon Magazine (up until his arrest for bank robbery – a colorful guy), recognized the car as one previously owned by his brother-in-law. I drove it for approximately a year and a half before wrecking it. A great deal of Bondo fell out of the bodywork, exposing lots of sheet metal damage that I hadn't been aware of.

I painted a comic-book "explosion" over the new damage. On the road, other Alfa drivers would honk at me. I'm still not certain if this was in camaraderie for another Alfa driver or in protest at the condition of my car, but I continued driving it until the clutch started slipping.

I was living in the basement of the Main Street Gallery, where I showed my paintings, when I met car racer Riley Hopkins. I related my idea of building a street able sprint car. Riley was enthused and offered to help. Somehow, this first involved lending him all my savings from truck driving so he could finish up a car project of his own.

The idea for the street able sprint car was inspired by the races I had attended with my dad at the Aurora Speedway. Midgets and sprint cars embodied the final incarnation of pre-wind tunnel aerodynamic styling.

Though all other forms of auto racing had long since evolved into wedges and inverted wings, the short tracks of American open wheel racing were the last to convert to modern aerodynamics. I liked the continuous modification too, whereas sports and formula racers tended to campaign their cars as they came from the factory and then buy a newer model when the old one was no longer competitive. In the American bull rings, drivers would modify their vehicles year after year, lengthening or 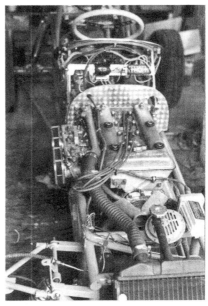 shortening them, growing new intakes, vents, exterior oil reservoirs, and adding clearance blisters to accommodate these mechanical changes. Ten-year-old cars were still viable winners having morphed into reliable "specials". The garish circus paint jobs and advertising appealed to me, too.

I wanted to build a car that looked like it had continued to morph until it became a commuter with auxiliary seating and pontoon fenders.

Ideally, I would have powered it with an Offenhauser

engine, the mighty mainstay of American open wheel racing for more than fifty years, but such an exotic engine was well beyond my means. I was willing to accept the Alfa engine as an available substitute that shared the alloy, four cylinder twin overhead cam layout of the Offenhauser. I later learned from Griffith Borgeson's book "The Golden Age of the American Race Car" that there was a direct lineage between the two. The early Peugeot Grand Prix cars inspired Harry Miller's engine design. Miller went bankrupt in the Depression, but his shop foreman, Fred Offenhauser, took over the business and renamed it "Offenhauser" and continued to produce the Miller designed engines.

A pair of "Millers" was campaigned in France and Italy by Leon Duray in 1929, where they consistently posted lap records. Following the Italian Grand Prix at Monza, these cars were purchased by Ettore Bugatti who incorporated their top end design features into his engines, which inspired the layout of the later Alfa Romeo engines.

In the new millennium, replica '50s A.J. Watson Indianapolis roadsters began appearing at vintage races, using Alfa Romeo engines for power in lieu of Offenhausers. Who'd have thought?

According to Evan Wilson in his book "Alfa Romeo Giulietta" (a gift from Colin Case); Alfa Romeo Spider Veloce serial number 131543813 was produced in 1958. An immediate discrepancy appeared. Wilson's meticulous log of serial numbers states that this number was assigned to one of the one thousand five hundred and fifty two Model 750D Spiders, rather than one of the eight hundred fifty seven Model 750F Veloce Spiders produced in Milan that year. Yet Keith Magnuson clearly identified the engine as a Veloce, or racing model – including 40 mm DCO3 Weber carburetors and specially balanced and hardened connecting rods. Since the matching serial numbers were stamped into the side of the block, it had to be the original engine. Additionally, the car did feature the "Veloce" emblem on the fender.

Engine builder Ralph Ghent, who prepared the head, discovered that the camshafts were unlike any others he had ever seen. Alfa Romeo camshafts are symmetrical with intake and exhaust cams being interchangeable. Timing marks are scribed 180 degrees apart so that they can be laid on either side of the head. But, these cams are uniquely scribed on one side only, identifying one as the intake and the other as the exhaust. It's possible that the engine had been modified by a previous owner for racing, but since Alfa Romeo re-tooled their factory for the 101 series engine in '59, it is also possible that a few transitional units were produced before the changeover was complete.

None of this did I know when I started my project. Having no idea how rare my car was, I dismembered the

Alfa, saving just the engine, drive train, rear axle, gauges, and the very cool Alfa badge from the nose of the crushed grill. The rest I gave to Seattle artist Clair Colquitt who built a three-wheeled pedal-powered ice cream cart out of the pieces. He later sold it to the Friedlander's of the jewelry business.

From Jerry Day's race car shop on Aurora Avenue, I purchased a fiberglass nose, tail and cowl for $140. These parts were already archaic for sprint car racing, the sport having moved on to wedge-shaped sheet aluminum bodies with exposed fuel tanks at the rear. Jerry must have known this when he sold me the parts. He asked if I was building a sprint or a modified. "I'm not building a race car" I mumbled, embarrassed to admit what I was up to.

I designed a tube space-frame and suspension based on my understanding of "Racing and Sports Car Chassis Design" by Michael Costin and David Phipps. I purchased  the hulk of a Triumph Spitfire from which I salvaged the front hub carriers, brake rotors and the fuel filler cap. A Honda Civic fuel tank turned sideways fit in the lower half of the tail leaving a potential small storage compartment above it. With a hack saw, a half-round file and great deal of determination, I cut and fish-mouthed the tubes for the frame laying them out on a full size plywood jig, mimicking the process I had used to build balsa aircraft models as a boy. When I had finished all the pieces, Riley brazed them together for me, teaching me how to braze in the process. This all took about two weeks. But, with no money I was unable to proceed.

After six months of trying to finish Riley's Pinto powered "Condor" for him, so I could get my money back (still waiting), I cut my losses and stored the Alfa Sprint Car frame and boxed parts in my parents' basement where they remained for the next twelve years. I moved to New York to pursue my wife to be, Jennifer, and a career as an illustrator.

In 1984, back in Seattle working as a graphic artist for the Seattle Engineering Department, I resumed work on the Alfa Special. My friend, Michael Murphy, had volunteered himself as caretaker of the dilapidated Alki Hotel on 5th Avenue. He used one of the three storefronts for a live-in studio space. I offered to split his rent for one of the remaining storefronts. All of the debris that we cleared from these two spaces we loaded into the third, now named the "The Rubble Room".

My parents were glad to be relieved of the project. Spreading out the pieces on the floor of the hotel, I found far more than I remembered. Many parts I had designed and redesigned and didn't recall actually building. Most of them bolted together smoothly. Suspension mounts I revised, cutting off the old ones and brazing on new mountings. I had purchased a new clutch from Grand Prix Motors back before I stored the project. Some of my early parts selections proved unsatisfactory, like a Pinto steering rack with cable U-joint and a Vega radiator. I replaced the steering rack with a Triumph unit and had Seattle Radiator construct a five row cooler that fit in the nose. I did my best to rebuild the difficult '58 Alfa gear box, but eventually replaced it with a more manageable '59 split case transmission purchased from Ralli-Round.

The engine, I took to Keith Magnuson's Alfa shop (Ralli-Round). Keith lit up when he saw the parts. A 750 series Veloce! He wanted to know if I was doing a full restoration of the car and I told him about Colquitt's ice cream cart. Keith put his head down on his desk and murmured "They all go different ways." But after a moment, he sat back up, "OK, I can help."

I couldn't help but notice that Keith had a 750 series Spider at the back of his shop that he was trying to restore. It was in a lot worse shape than the one I'd cut up.

Keith hot tanked the block and head for me. Magna-fluxing revealed that three of the four precious Veloce connecting rods were cracked. Using later 101 series rods (thicker, but the same throw length), Keith machined a set down to 750 series specs, shot hardened them, and then balanced them, creating a new set of 750 Veloce rods. A &

W Machine reground and balanced the crankshaft, proudly engraving their name on one of the counterweights. I bought Borge forged aluminum domed pistons, Swedish chrome rings, new cast iron cylinders, new valves and guides, a new timing chain, and bearings.

The block had suffered from some previous owner's amateurish adaptation of a homemade oil cooler to the engine. A pair of SAE bolts had been forced into the metric threads that had located the filter mount. Ralph Ghent welded up the damaged bolt holes and re-tapped them to original specs with heli-coils.

Keith borrowed a rare 750 Series Shop Manual from the Durante brothers of Tacoma, so I could Xerox a copy for myself. I took the parts home to a house I rented on East Marion. There, I carefully assembled the engine in an up-

stairs bedroom while Jennifer was busy giving birth to Leila, our first child, in another bedroom. Leila grew up to be feisty and would eventually graduate Summa-cum-laude from NYU. I built a car for her when she was five, but that's another story.

The alloy twin overhead cam engine was just within my capacity to lift and carry. When it was finished, I took it to the hotel storefront where the rest of the car was stored and installed it in the frame.

I browsed junkyards and motorcycle shops for parts. I shaped a teardrop pontoon cycle fender mold to echo the tail. Damien Gregory, the famous custom motorcycle builder, helped me with the fiberglass casting which we did in one of the upstairs rooms of the hotel. Damien also located two pairs of Harley Davidson coil shocks for me. I found a set of matching black louvered panels at Pacific Industrial Salvage. Picking them up, I realized they were aluminum. I adapted them to my body panels. Headlight buckets, tail lights, and mirrors came from Bent Bike salvage and Downtown Harley Davidson. I fabricated a grill from a sign that said "Left Lane Only". Some of the orange reflective paint is still visible on the undersides of the grill vanes. Zappfe Silversmiths polished this part to a chrome-like finish.

A parking lot across the street from the hotel provided a testing space where a few early problems were sorted out, like a throttle that jammed open due to insufficient clearance. Other parts took years to fail. Modeled after racing car technology, some of my suspension members were adequate for smooth tracks and limited mileage, but when faced with potholes  and daily driving, it was obvious that they needed reinforcement.

An invitation to exhibit my Alfa as part of a "Cars by Artists" show at the Bellevue Art Museum in February of '98 provided sufficient impetus for a frame up rebuild. I took this opportunity to do a lot of small upgrades, like relocating body mounting tabs, improving accessibility and cleaning up the wiring. New paint, Red Number 48 DuPont Centari Acrylic Enamel (code WT-4171), was applied by Jim at Jim's Crash Shop. Greg Nowak sprayed the frame with Rustoleum Smoke Gray Gloss. Walter De Marsh of Mobetta

Shoes fashioned the upholstery from Boeing Surplus first class 747 seat leather supplied by Kim Hall. I built several sets of exhaust headers before I came up with a design and exhaust note that satisfied me. The final version featured  equal lengths gathered in counter clockwise firing order to create a vortex draught. Skilled sheet metal worker Mike Howe re-skinned the side car with Boeing surplus sheet aluminum using my original panels for templates, improving the fit as he went. Kim Hall showed me how to put a machine turned finish on the dashboard and firewall and set me up with the tools to do it. With Mike, Kelly Green and Lynn Taylor's help, we worked straight through the night before the show and finished with just two hours to spare. I jumped in and headed to Bellevue. There it was; done and parked, gleaming in a museum! As the last owner of almost every car I've ever had, I was relieved that this project had made it intact into a museum exhibit.

Of course, I keep tinkering with it. Adding chrome trim to the cowling, a Brooklands windshield to the sidecar, a Bosche starter and such.

Idling at a stop light, a truck pulled up next to me and the driver rolled down his window: "What is it?" he asked.

"Alfa Romeo" I gave him the short answer.

"No" he said, "it isn't. I'm the president of the Northwest Alfa Romeo Club. That's not an Alfa Romeo."

OK, I admitted, I'd built it out of an Alfa Romeo.

He invited me out to the track, Seattle International Raceway, for their Club racing day.

The Scrutineer asked me if I was actually going to run

it with the side car. "Of course, it's the only one here!" I exclaimed.

On the track, the little engine would wind up to nearly 8000 rpm, topping out around 120 mph in fourth gear. The lightweight car, just 1140 pounds, gripped well in the corners despite hard street tires. As I gathered my nerve, I went faster through the turns on each successive lap until, at last, I was no longer braking anywhere on the track except at the end of the long straight and at the bottom of the hill diving into the S turns. The atrocious street handling was just the car's disinclination to go straight at a constant speed. Loaded up on three wheels (four counting the side car), one front tire waving in the air, it tracked pretty well. I sensed that the near equal fore-and-aft weight distribution I had created made the grip and balance precarious; cornering sharply, but likely to let go on all at once if it lost adhesion. The car might be a real racer in the hands of a more talented driver than me. I also had to admit that while I could design and build fully adjustable suspension, I really had no idea how to tune the suspension and to this day find it easier to learn to drive what I have rather than figure out how to adjust it. Future education.

The side car was an issue. Not the side car's tire adhesion, which was negligible, but the inertia of its asymmetric weight. I needed to anticipate the side car's momentum, steering slightly into it on braking and away from it on acceleration.

A club member was running his Lamborghini Diablo at the same time. He blew past me on the long straight but I found that I was catching him through the winding turns. Tempted to press for a little more top end down the front straight, the head gasket let go.

In the pits, I was approached first by a turn marshal who thanked me for "letting us hear the engine". It was a lovely note coming from the elaborate exhaust and then Fritz Durnburger, the celebrated Alfa Romeo restorer, introduced himself. Fritz wanted my carburetors.

The DCO3 Weber's, manufactured only in 1958, were difficult to maintain, had no choke for starting, and had quickly been superseded by the upgraded model DCOE. Fritz took my number and called me the following Monday. He offered a new set of DCOE Weber's, the manifold to match them to my engine, and $500. I figured the only thing rarer than my carburetors would be the guy looking for them. I took the deal.

On a later trip to the track, a turn marshal wanted to ride in the side car. The extra weight was too much and I spun off the course in turn nine. It was more excitement than I think he was looking for.

The tiny jewel-like engine, just 1290 cc displacement (about 76 cubic inches) but now with modern 40 mm DCOE Weber's, balanced piston and rods, and a very custom vortex exhaust, is undoubtedly the most powerful antique 750 series Veloce engine in existence. At least until somebody should turbocharge one. But, that's most likely to be me.

I sold advertising space on the car in the manner of race cars. It looked appropriate, legitimized it for the police, and helped pay for the project.

The first sponsor was Trattoria Mitchelli Restaurant, which bought a space before I had finished the car. Later, Ralli Round, Lava Lounge, Ghent Machine Service, Nightingale Dance Company, Grey Top Cab, Close Enough Engineering, and Hiroshi's Restaurant were added. It's a good advertising deal. People are constantly taking photos of it, whether parked or going down the road.

When my daughters were small, they would occasionally ask me to pick them up from school or ballet class in the "Red Car". I was glad to oblige. Later, when youngest daughter Alisa was in high school, she hesitated about getting into the side car. "Is this safe?" she asked. No honey, of course it isn't. Sometimes, if it's sunny, I can get Jennifer to take a cruise with me, but more often I ride alone and the side car gets my brief case.

I get pulled over from time to time by the cops, but it's always because they want to admire the car and tell me about the '32 Ford that they're building.

When I drive it to observe the vintage car races, I usually get waved into the pits. If I drive it to an art show opening and there's no parking, I can pull it up onto the sidewalk and the meter maids assume it's part of the show.

When I drove it to the Dirt Cup, the county police officer attending the gate invited me to park directly in front of the main entrance. He even volunteered to watch it for me. "Shouldn't this be in the infield?" he asked.

It's such an unusual car that I can go to an Italian car show and suck the crowd away from the "real" cars. They've seen Ferraris and Maseratis before. Experts will stand next to it and authoritatively tell their buddies about when Alfa Romeo built these and where they were raced.

I was in a Sea Fair parade when I ran into Smith's brother-in-law working as a photographer. "Remember your old Alfa?" I asked him. "This is it."

I like to just do the speed limit and stay in the slow lane to allow people to admire my car and then pass me. It's a good commuter. People let me merge in front of them so they can check out the vehicle. If I park on the street, I will return to find some enthusiast who has interrupted their day to guard my car for me.

Driving my work van, I may occasionally get the finger from other drivers, but in the Alfa I always get the thumb.

Body Shop Adventures

by Dave Alvar

In 1969, after I got out of the Army, I got a job as the "Assistant Manager" of a body shop at a Pontiac dealership. Mostly, this meant that I chased parts, swept floors, and answered phones. Eventually, I learned to write estimates, which made me feel more important.

One day a very tall, muscular black gentleman brought his new Grand Prix SJ in for an estimate. Someone had sideswiped it. The damage wasn't severe, but it did involve a lot of sheet metal and trim. I wrote the estimate and we got the job.

The repairs were completed in a few days and new paint was expertly applied. The only problem was that the side trim was back-ordered and we had no choice but to wait for it.

A week passed; then two. The tall, muscular gentleman was growing ever more impatient to get his car back. He called frequently and it got to the point where I dreaded answering the phone.

Finally, the trim arrived. It was quickly installed and I had one of the lot boys give the car a deluxe detailing. He parked the glistening auto in front of my office and I immediately got on the phone to give the owner the good news.

While I was on the phone, I noticed a huge tow truck backing up to an impounded car at the far upper end of the lot. The driver got out and started hooking up the cables. I hung up the phone and started doing paperwork. Sudden movement caught my attention. I looked up and saw the tow truck and the impounded car racing across the lot and I thought, "That driver is going way too fast". That's when I noticed that the driver was actually running along behind the rig, trying desperately to catch it. It took just a moment for the lumbering tow truck to cross the lot and broadside the Grand Prix. I jumped up and stood there open-mouthed as I watched that beautiful car become a twisted mass of metal.

A few minutes later, the tall, muscular, and now very angry, gentleman arrived. I pointed to the tow truck driver and said, "Talk to him. He did it".

I remember when the dealership got in its first Firebird Trans Am. It was a white beauty with blue racing stripes. Unfortunately, it arrived with a small dent in the door. Naturally, it came directly to the body shop to have that blemish corrected. Our paint shop was a few blocks from the body shop and, typically, I had the privilege of shuttling the cars back and forth. I was about a block down the street, sitting at a red light, when I got the brilliant idea of lighting up those big rear tires. When the light turned green, I revved up the engine and dumped the clutch. Imagine my surprise when I discovered that I was in reverse! I hit the brake and clutch pedals and brought the car to a stop about an inch from the front bumper of a garbage truck. I drove it ever so carefully after that.

At some point, the dealership started selling a tiny little car known as the Subaru 360. It looked like an egg on wheels and had suicide doors. One of those doors came open on I-5 and the result was something like Humpty Dumpty. The car was hauled to the shop where it was quickly declared to be a total loss. A few of us were standing around looking at the remains when one genius suggested that we lift it as high as we coul, and drop it. Of course, the rest of us thought that was a splendid idea. It turned out to not be all that heavy; about 1,000 pounds and we managed to press it over our heads. On the count of three, we dropped it and ran for our lives. Good thing we ran, because it didn't exactly bounce straight back up.

The dealership also tried selling the Yugo briefly. Not too many folks wanted them, no matter how inexpensive they were. We got one in the body shop with the driver's door all bent out of shape. Turned out the guy slammed the door on the seatbelt buckle, and that's what did all the damage. Probably a good thing they didn't do crash testing back then. These things would not have fared well.

We had one body man who did excellent work, but spoke very little English. After repairing some rear end damage to a late model Catalina, he installed the letters across the deck lid ... P O T I N A C. We had a hard time explaining to him why that was funny.

There was one old body man who, in his spare time, liked to rebuild wrecks behind the shop. He picked up a '66 or '67 Nova that had been hit hard in the front. He bought a complete front clip and grafted it on. One morning, one of the other guys walked in the back door, chuckling, and told me to go out and check out the Nova. From a distance, it looked great. Then I got closer, and noticed that something wasn't quite right. I sighted along the side of the car, from back to front. There was a jog at the firewall, and the entire front end was aimed slightly to the right of where it should be. The Nova went away a few days later. Not sure what he did with it, but for a while there, I kept an eye out for a Nova dog-walking down the road.

Another body man was a young, blond, surfer-dude type of guy. His daily driver was a very decent, totally original '56 Nomad. One day a guy offered him $1,500 cash for it. He sent the guy packing and announced that the car

132

would be worth way more than that someday. I thought he was crazy. Shows how much I knew.

One day a wrecker brought in a beautiful, fully-loaded, Bonneville that had been totaled. My boss looked it over and then told me to check out the odometer. It had a grand total of seven miles on it. The couple who bought it was on their way home from the dealership when someone ran a light. Fortunately, they fared better than the car did.

Another time, an attractive young woman brought in a nice '67 GTO with a lot of undercarriage damage. She reluctantly explained that she'd had a bit too much to drink one night and tried, unsuccessfully, to jump a rather large curb. The next morning, it occurred to her that her boyfriend was going to be less than pleased. Since it was his car and he was due to come home from the Army in a few days, she was pretty anxious to get it repaired.

And then there was the bright orange GTO Judge that came in to the shop. We repaired it and gave it back to the owner. But, he wasn't happy, so he returned it to us, about ten times. I think he was still bringing it back when I quit working there. Some folks are just hard to please.

Bronx Dreamer

by Mike Trinagel

Can you remember back to when you first started fantasizing about cars?

I began daydreaming, at a very young age, about the type of cars I could see myself driving, imagining that I would be the one to build them to fit the dreams, and recall my first one like it was yesterday.

I was living on Hone Avenue in the Da Bronx, NY and by 12 years old, everybody knew I was a car guy. I had been learning my craft and building my skills in my father's backyard and garage for a few years by the time a '65 Vista Cruiser wagon caught my eye on the way to junior high school one morning. It wasn't so much the car itself, but the design of the raised glass panels on the roof that captured my imagination and wouldn't let go.

To say this car was neglected would be an understatement. I would walk by it on my way to school every day and see this car parked in front of "the projects", noticing that it was only moved on "alternate side of the street parking days" for street cleaning in the Bronx. The paint was faded and the dash was sun cracked. The tires were low and it was filled with "stuff". Yet, seeing this car was the highlight of my daily walks. I would have never guessed this car was so loved by its owner!

I quietly stalked this car all through junior high, leaving notes on the windshield for the owner to please call me so I could buy the car. One day on my way to school, I saw the owner. It was my chance to talk to this man about letting me buy his car. Unfortunately, that meeting didn't work out the way I had hoped. He didn't want to talk about it. The car wasn't for sale.

He was the original owner and had driven the car off the showroom floor. While it didn't look like it, this car was his baby and he was not ready to even think of selling it. He did promise to let me know if he decided it was time to let it go. As it turned out, he took a LONG time to think about it!

While I waited to hear from him, I continued working in my father's backyard; washing cars, learning some bodywork from my neighbor Johnny, working on different projects and, ONLY because I had to, going to school. And I waited... and waited some more! I dreamt of that Oldsmobile Vista Cruiser Wagon all through junior high and right up into my second semester at Christopher Columbus High School. Then, I finally got the call. The owner was ready to talk to me again. It had been almost three years of watching that car on a daily basis and in that time my brain had created many visions of what it could be.

When we met, he shared with me how attached he was to the car, but he felt I would give it a good home and take care of it. With tears in his eyes, he said that he knew I didn't have a lot of money so he was going to let me buy it for $200. This was quite the turn of events and a sudden change of heart for him. I knew the car was worth about $2000. I couldn't believe how this was working out. I went from dreamer to owner in an afternoon.

The glass that had originally caught my eye had kept my wheels turning. I had all kinds of ideas of what to do to this car. It had become an obsession. I'd always had trouble in school and was not the most popular, so I found my peace working and creating. I wasn't able to absorb the materials the teachers taught in the classroom due to what is now recognized as ADD or ADHD, which back then was seen as simply being defiant and disrespectful. So, I was always put in with the troubled kids. This made learning even harder. I decided to drop out of school and devote all of my time to creating my vision of this car.

I had everything set up in my father's garage, including my beloved stereo. I had to have my music! Working on the car for about nine months straight, I would come out to eat, sleep, and help my father and my Uncle Chaim by doing chores so they could relax when they got home from work. I especially loved the winter and doing snow removal for them. This was my way of showing them how much they meant to me. I was a perfectionist, making sure every speck of snow was removed. These guys worked so hard and I loved them so much that I didn't want them to have to even think about doing this when they got home. Uncle Chaim lived right down the block, so it was my routine to go take care of his house as soon as I finished my parent's.

I had always kind of been the odd man out at school. Even in my own home, my older brother literally hated me and took great pleasure in torturing me. So, I found peace working in a classroom that I understood … the garage! This car had put so many visions in my head that I would get lost while working and creating.

I didn't welcome very many to visit while I was working, but when my Uncle Chaim would come over to check on me and whatever project I was working on, I always felt very loved and supported. I enjoyed seeing that look of pride on his face as he just watched me, absorbing every move I made. Many times, we didn't even speak for hours while he watched me work. Sometimes, I would even forget he was there! I loved making him proud and to this day, often think about my life and wonder if he would still be proud of me. I miss him so much; even when he would grab my jaw and give me a big ol' wet bite on the cheek with a hug, his signature sign of affection.

I had gone into the garage when I started working on this car at 6'1" and 285 pounds. I was now 95 pounds lighter and felt  like a new man with the confidence that had grown since letting my shop skills explode and seeing my vision of this car become a reality.

Once, the garage door was open while I was working and I noticed our tenant's babysitter watching me, occasionally making flirting glances my way. Even though she was paying attention to me, I still had a bit of fear, as most young guys that age do. I was afraid that she might just be toying with me and would reject me if I returned her advances. That fear passed and I enjoyed her company. Spending more time with the babysitter, I saw that I could make time for relationships in addition to creating my dreams.

I still preferred to cruise solo, though. As long as I had my car and my music, I was in heaven. The babysitter was simply an occasional, but welcome, distraction.

I had cut out the center of the roof of the car, so now I had the four panels originally on the roof and an entire center panel of smoked glass. In the end, everything had a custom cut. I designed teardrop side windows, head-lights, taillights, turn signals, and sealed up the back hatch, adding a diamond shaped window and an opening like a casket would slide into.

My father's contribution to this dream was cutting custom solid mahogany running boards finished in polyurethane that fit into the slots I had prepared. I built a  center console out of plywood from my dad's garage and put in a wicked stereo system made by Jensen, an addition I was proud of because it was considered high end back in the day. To set it all off, I carpeted the entire car. Floors, sides, dashboard... it was shag heaven! I even had mohair on the headliner areas that weren't glass and added a chromed out chained steering wheel. I still didn't have a lot of money at this point, so this beast lived in flat black. It was BAD ASS and I called it "The Monster".

The car became a part of the 1970's art that I had envisioned since riding to the Catskills with my father before I could even drive. This was the first car that I could legally drive and I was now able to cruise through the mountains of the Catskill Region of New York on my own. I was fulfilling my wildest dreams.

That car was so wicked and I was so anxious to cruise that I would head to the Catskills to meet friends that were waiters and busboys at midnight after they got off work. We would park atop a hill and sit around the car just zoning out as "The Monster" sat eerily in the moonlight with the evening fog settling in around it. The flat black made it look like it was truly in its element.

My friends would talk about their day at work and the various customers and incidents that had happened. All the while, the stereo kept in tune with our "calm" playing Pink Floyd, Led Zeppelin, Emerson Lake & Palmer, and whatever else the mood called for. This car solidified my identity as "the one who could create whatever his mind could see".

My passion for music, cars, and women has never changed. It has only been enhanced. I still see cars that catch my eye and have to make them mine to restore or recreate. The memories of this first car take me to a place where my whole world was changed and hope everyone's memories of their first builds are as vivid as mine. Of course, owning my own body shop helps to make my dreams possible.

Holly Hanging and Other Adventures

by Dale Moreau

Newfane Central High School in western New York State was a fun place to be in the 1950s. There were many activities to participate in, many of them involving the opposite sex. During the winter holiday season, one of the functions was for each class to decorate the lockers in their area of the school. It was called "Holly Hanging" and at the time was a popular competition, mostly between the freshman and sophomores. It was considered un-cool by some in the upper classes.

My class won twice while I was there. In my freshman year, they announced that the seniors of 1960 were the winners and we realized that in four years that would be us! We were a little better tuned in the next year, but I was sidetracked by other pursuits and didn't hear the results until later.

That other pursuit was a girl. She was in the class one year ahead of me and had a smoldering sexuality about her that just came naturally. She was a tall, quiet girl with medium blond hair and was usually in white blouses, full long skirts and saddle shoes. It was a stunning combination that always caught my attention whenever she was near.

For some strange reason, she liked me and would sit by me on the bus trip home after school. Sometimes, I would be looking out the window and not see her come on the bus. I would feel a hand slide inside my coat and I knew she had arrived. Her father was the head of the Boy Scouts and they lived in a nice Craftsman style house in Ridgewood, New York, about a mile from me on the old Ellicott road. We would have interesting conversations and sometimes I would get invited to get off at her house to have some hot chocolate and cookies that her mother seemed to always have just sitting around.

One day, just after classes let out, a bunch of us were putting the finishing touches on the decorations of our lockers for the Holly Hanging contest. I was sitting on the floor taping on some crate paper when I felt someone very close to me. I looked up and there she was. Before I could say anything, she planted a very nice wet kiss on me, smiled, and simply walked away.

We had some kind of thing going on the bus which ended up with her owing me kiss and me always trying to get her to pay up. Well, that was such a down payment that if she never paid the full amount, I still would have been happy. It impressed me enough that fifty years later I still remember that very moment.

On the bus ride home, she asked if I was going to the football game the next day. I said I would, but didn't have a way to get there. She offered to take me with her. Her dad had a new '57 Plymouth that was a typical family car, so that didn't excite me much, but the idea of her picking me up for the game did. It was a great, fall afternoon for early December and showing up with her really raised my status with the "in crowd".

One, it blew away the guys in my class that an "older woman" liked me, because the girls in my class always went with the older guys and the opposite hardly ever happened. Two, it helped keep the eighth grade girls from bugging me so much. I would be out on the ball field and they would be singing a popular song that included "Dao" that they changed to Dale … and it ruined my concentration. On the other hand, it was a good excuse for me to cover up the fact that I couldn't hit the ball past the pitcher.

Cars have always been part of my life and in high school they were very important. At times, cars even involved the teachers. Sometimes, the teachers that were the toughest in the classroom were the ones that students wound up thinking were the coolest.

My math teacher was a car guy and really got me interested in British sports cars. His name was Winston Rabadue and he owned a red '55 Austin Healey and had a Dalmatian dog that went everywhere with him. He was quite a dapper guy with black wavy hair and a British style mustache. He wore the proper sports car cap, had a rather classic air about him, and was quite the ladies' man. He had a smart mouth, too. We were friends off campus, but in class he called me Moron instead of Moreau and, I'm afraid, with some credibility.

Agnes B. Klock was another story. She was a rather formidable woman who ruled over the Biology department. She even had a sign taped over the clock in her class room that said "you're watching the wrong clock". On some late afternoons, after ball practice, the guys would meet at their cars outside of school. If the parking lot was full, you nosed in against the curb, meaning you had to back out to into the street and then drive away. This gave some of them a very good excuse to back up farther than they had to, drop the transmission into low, and burn rubber all the way to the corner. This was called "laying a patch". Then, they would all get out and see who laid the longest patch. One day, as they were holding just such a contest, out came Mrs. Klock. It was "oh shit" time. Or so they thought. Mrs. Klock owned a '56 Ford Ranch Wagon with a 292 ci V-8 engine that came from the factory with dual exhausts that sounded very good. The silence was deafening as she got into the wagon, fired up the V-8, backed out and laid a patch all the way to the corner. Everyone was yelling and saying "OK Mrs. Klock", but all had the wisdom to never bring up the subject in class.

Our science teacher was Mr. Haley. I, for one, can tell you that the stories about guys reading car magazines in class are all true. I was one of those guys and when Mr. Haley caught me one day, he grabbed the magazine from me and ripped it in half. The next day he told me to stay after class. He had bought another one just like it and gave it to me. He just needed to make a point.

Another thing about cars in high school ... When you took Drivers Education you could get a license sooner and it lowered your insurance payments a bunch. After watching the usual gory movie about teen agers killing themselves, you went out to get actual experience behind the wheel. The car provided by the local Ford dealer was a cheap four door model with a stick shift and a six cylinder engine. The one thing it had that no other car on the road had was an extra set of pedals on the passenger side for the teacher. If a student driver lost control of the clutch or brakes, the teacher could take over and get the car stopped.

There was a girl in my sophomore class with an older brother who had already graduated several years before. He had been in several car accidents and actually had a metal plate in his head from one of them. Late one night, he came down the Gooding Street hill in Lockport with his foot mashed down hard on the gas pedal of his '57 Ford four door hard top. Remember, it is a four door hard top. At the bottom of the hill was a long sweeping left turn going past Reed's Hot Dog Stand and the Odd Fellows home. When he made that turn, he was "haulin' ass".

At that moment, the local cops were filling up on hot dogs at Reed's and they flipped on their lights to give chase. The road went downhill again past the Windom Lawn Home, then up and curved again to the left at the Niagara County Fairgrounds. In 1957, there was a long row of Poplars running a good half a mile along the road on the right. As he attempted to make the second curve, now with the police on his tail, the car began to slide and hit one of the tall slim trees at about 70 miles an hour. The crash was explosive and tore the car in half. The impact sent his body sliding down the pavement and a steel plate wasn't going to help this time.

I went down to Wright's Corners the next day to view the car in the back lot of the local Edsel dealer where the wrecker took the pieces. There sat the whole front of the car, cut in half just behind the front seat and now appeared to be a convertible. I reached in and turned on the key, the gas gauge read half full even though the tank was in the twisted and severed back half of the car.

Reed's was and still is the place to get hamburgers, hot-dogs, and milkshakes. You could drive up with your car, BS with your buddie,s and check out the other cars and girls. At the time, the prices were all 25 cents; as was the gallon of gas to get there. Reed's was on the edge of town, but downtown Lockport had three places for a kid to go after school.

On the east end, where the "In crowd" hung out, was Castle's Dairy. It was where the Vandemark kids would drive up and down Main Street, picking up girls as they cruised in their black '56 Olds ragtop.

Dougie Castle was a third or fourth generation Castle that lived around the corner from me in late 1956 before we moved to the country. He lived in a very traditional brick home on Willow Ave. just down the street from the

Vandemark mansion. The house was set well back from the street with a nice long, straight, paved driveway.

Dougie's mom had bought a new '53 Buick Skylark convertible. It was still like new, with low miles, in that spring of 1956. The car was spectacular with its silver paint, white top, and red leather interior. We were in the 8th grade at Emmet Belknap School and would run the four blocks home to his house.

His mom would give him the keys and we would drive up and down the 200 foot drive way honking at girls like Maureen O'Brian, the doctor's kid, as she was walking home to her house just down the street. She now sells real estate in Lockport and I see signs with her name on them all over town.

Just across the street was the large white clapboard house of the manager of the two Harrison Radiator plants in Lockport. After school, his son would invite some guys over to play table tennis and pool on the side porch and drink lemonade from crystal glasses. In June, the strawberry festival was held out at the fair grounds and I was invited to go along with them. His dad had two new company cars and I was to ride in the '56 Olds 98 four door hard top. It was red and white with a Wonder Bar radio and Air Conditioning. I rode shot gun and hung my arm out the window and when the window suddenly started to go up I was shocked. I had never seen power windows before.

Then there were the two other "hang outs", as well. In the middle of Main Street was the Royal. It had a lunch counter and sold ice cream and was known to be the place where the bad kids hung out. Of course, I was never in there.

Down at the big bridge on Main Street was The Crystal. It was run for over forty years by Jimmie Shummas, who didn't let any rowdy goings on happen in his place. Our family would go there on Saturday night and my choice off the menu was always a toasted cheese sandwich and a chocolate milkshake. The chocolate milkshake was actually made with vanilla ice cream, Phosphate soda water, and chocolate syrup and they had to get that right or it just wasn't any good.

My mom was born in 1909 and went to The Crystal on her first date in the '20s and I took Barbara Saxton there on my first date thirty-some years later. The ice cream was homemade and the decor was old English with tin ceilings, dark wood booths, bent wood chairs, and ice cream tables. We had a lot of good times with Jimmie as I was growing up in the 1950s.

We lived on Pine Street which was kind of the poor neighbors of a very rich area of old Lockport. Another school friend lived two blocks up the street where the houses began to get a lot bigger and nicer. His last name, Bewley, is an old and well known Lockport family name that is still on a large building on Main Street in Lockport. Their dark brick house, set well back from the street, was large enough to have a half-court basketball arena in the attic. After all the girls had passed the Castle residence we would go over to the Bewley residence and shoot baskets while the maid put together tuna sandwiches and Cokes.

About this same time we decided it was time to paint my friend Buzz's '38 Ford coupe. His dad worked at the lumber yard and they sold paint too. So he gave us a gross of 1½ oz. bottles of black touch up paint, each with its own brush. It took us a week and a half to do the job and we thought it was really cool. We then graduated to bug spray guns with paint instead of bug poison and we turned pro with his mom's Electro Lux vacuum cleaner with the hose stuck in the other end, a technique used by many back in those early hot rodding days.

Buzz's poor mom had six kids of her own and the friends of all of them that were there on a daily basis. She fed us all on baloney and cheese sandwiches, a far cry from the other guy's houses just a few blocks away.

Life was good then. We all got along no matter which side of the tracks we lived on and the whole thing that tied us together was the cars. It is still true today and it has provided me with a vocation, great times with cars, and most importantly lifelong friends.

Oh, and Buzz still lives in Lockport. His sister bought the old house and fixed it up and we are friends to this day.

Asphalt Eating Olds

by David Dickinson

In 1968, I bought my second car. It was a 1954 Oldsmobile 88 two-door sedan with a big powerful V8 and a smooth as pudding automatic transmission.

I bought that car for $85. It had a beautiful interior and a faded yellow paint job. The seats were all intact and clean and the dash shined like new. Knowing what I know now and having much more patience and appreciation for all things old and in need of just a little TLC, I probably could have gotten the paint to look fairly nice, too. The body was straight as an arrow, with no rust or dents and the metal was as thick as a nickel. Even the chrome was nice and shiny.

I have no idea how many miles it had on it, but I would go to the gas station, fill the oil, and check the gas. I'm pretty sure it had a bad main seal. At the time, gas was about 29 cents a gallon and oil was a quarter. I thought the exhaust sounded pretty cool, but in reality, it was quite simply worn out and louder than it had been when it was younger.

The original knee action shocks were bad. 1954 was the last year for the "knuckle" shocks, expensive to replace even then, and the car literally rode like a boat on the open ocean. A couple of my friends swore they got seasick in it one night but, I think it might have had something to do with the "barley pop" that they had been drinking.

When I laid down my money, the Olds was only 14 years old and had had only one owner... the proverbial little old lady, a friend of my grandmother. It was far from being the classic that it is today and just a cheap car that I could drive and not worry about too much. In today's world, it had what is considered a nice patina and would have been a great candidate for an easy restoration. In 1968, it was simply a beater.

When I first got that behemoth of a sled, unbeknownst to me, it had a broken motor mount. Being just a young punk with little real car experience, I thought it might be cool to see how much rubber I could burn by running it in reverse and slamming it into drive. Well, the long and short of it was that the sudden change of direction and torque caused the motor to jump violently around in the engine compartment. Amazingly, it caused no serious damage, other than shattering the shift linkage that ran through the steering column. The tranny was fine, but I suddenly had a free-floating gearshift handle. So, I went down to the local parts store to get a floor shifter for it. They didn't have one for a '54, so I got one for a '55. Hey, the cars looked pretty similar on the outside.

Working full time, in addition to going to high school, I didn't have time to work on it. I wasn't in auto shop at the time, so I took it to the local mechanic up the street from the high school and he said, "No problem, I can install it. I'll do it for $35." He agreed that there shouldn't be much difference in the shift linkage from one year to the next. After all, the cars did look pretty similar... for the most part.

Well, after a couple of days of being put off, I was kind of upset that he hadn't finished it and I went to give him an earful. The long and short of it was that he had to heat each linkage bar and reshape them. It turns out that the '55 linkage wasn't anything like the '54, despite how similar the cars looked on the outside. Not only that, but being the conscientious mechanic that he was, he felt it only right that he give me back the car with the shift indicator on the dash working properly.

When all was said and done, I got my car back and it had a floor shifter that worked really smoothly with an operable shift indicator. A very cool unit! He spent a bunch of hours on it and he still only charged me the originally quoted $35. From that day on, that old boy was my mechanic… right up until he went out of business.

I was the envy of everyone for having scored on my install. The linkage never failed to operate smoothly and it was the best transaction I have ever had with a mechanical repair business.

One day, I planned on getting four new tires for the Olds after school. I mentioned that to a couple of friends and they both expressed disappointment that I hadn't quite burned off all the rubber on the tires it had. It was decided that I should remedy that situation prior to leaving school. So, with less common sense than a teenager usually displays, and once again proving what my dad used to say, "You don't have the sense to pour piss out of a boot…" I pulled into the senior parking lot.

Now, the new senior parking lot was not the least conspicuous place to do a burnout, but it had speed bumps. I pulled up to one of the pristine motion inhibitors in the newly asphalted lot and placed my back tires on the leading edge. The goal was to burn off as much rubber as I could before heading to the tire store, so I placed one foot on the brake and one on the gas. I pressed down on the gas just enough to get the tires turning and kept the brake pressed just enough to keep the car from moving. Once started, I gave it more gas and watched the smoke start to fill the area around my beater Olds.

It seemed like I was doing the longest burnout in motoring history. In reality, it was for a short time, but I generated a lot of smoke. In fact, there was so much smoke, and enough wind, that before too long the administration building was engulfed in tire smoke.

Not oblivious to the fact that what I was doing was against school policy, the law, and the most basic of common sense, I let off the gas and let the car roll to a parking space where I left it to smolder, so to speak. The smoke from the burnout lingered, wafting out of the wheels wells, incriminating the car in the nefarious event.

I had gotten out and walked away, watching from a distance as the police arrived. They inspected it, made some notes, looked around … and left. I guess they had bigger fish to fry than investigating a burnout where they couldn't prove who had done it.

To this day, I can't tell you why nothing came of it, but I was never called in, held accountable, or contacted at any time. There could have been serious repercussions, but the only long-term result was the one-inch divot in the speed bump where I had chewed away the asphalt. I left a short while later to go get tires before heading to work. The speed bump remained permanently scarred. I know because I went and looked at it many years later, surprised at how deep the mark still was.

I drove that car for what seemed like a long time. As I recall now, however, it was only for a few months before I found a cooler car that I just had to have and so I sold the Olds for $75. I'd have to guess that it's worth probably a couple hundred times more than that now and "Yes, I wish I still had it!"

Maybe that '54 Olds is floating around still, granted a new life by someone older and wiser than I was then, and with more money and appreciation for the fine old lady that she was. I often look for her at the local car shows, checking for telltale signs I may have left behind, like the 8 ball on the end of the tall floor mounted shifter.

If you see her, tell her I miss her and appreciate her more today than I ever did then. Just like all of the other old iron that I left behind from the days of my youth.

Has Anybody Seen My Old Friend Mike?

by Jim Muckenfuhs

I have owned many cool cars over the years. Like many old car guys that have come before me, I love the thrill of the hunt with the looking and inspecting, and talking with owners. But, I'm always itching for the next car and the next experience of that hunt and ultimate score.

1975 was a real high point in my driving experience. I got my driver's license and with it, I could finally get wheels of my own. My first car was a '71 Plymouth Duster. It had the 340cid V8 with a 4 barrel carb and ran well enough to get me into drag racing on the street at that tender young age of 16.

At my parent house, my bedroom consisted of a dresser, a small desk that held my cheap fold-up record player and a bed. Oh yeah, and a big ass set of drums, which I sold to buy the Duster. I'm sure the neighbors rejoiced.

In 1976, I had entered vocational school at Northwest High School in Cincinnati, Ohio. Auto Mechanics was a two year class and I made some great friends, including Mike. Next door to us was the body shop, the welding shop, and then the cosmetology class, which was, of course, all girls. Woohoo!

I didn't know it then, but I would meet my future wife in that class. We both graduated in '77. I went to work in a Toyota dealership and eventually spent almost 25 years as a mechanic at various places. Most of my career was with Nissan, but I worked many other places, also. All of my jobs involved working on imports. Triumphs, Volvos, Jaguars, Porches… you name it. That's where the money was back then.

Now, I don't recommend what my buddy, Mike, and I did to young drivers these days, but it worked really well for us. Keep in mind, the police back then didn't have all the radios, helicopters, and just sheer numbers they do today. You couldn't get away with what we did back then in today's world.

We were in a hurry to get home one night in the Duster and I was moving at a pretty good pace on a two-lane road. I passed a cop going in the other direction and in my rear view mirror I saw him whip around and hit his lights. So, I made a quick left into a neighborhood. I had a bit of a head start on him and I turned right and hit the gas at the first street I came to. Several houses down the street, I noticed a guy standing in his driveway washing his van. It was customized and had a nice paint job; the kind that was so popular back then. These were all split-level houses with two car garages. I noticed both garage doors were open and I took a shot. I whipped into his driveway and prayed there wasn't another car in the garage. There wasn't. I flew right past him as he was hosing the soap off and pulled right into his garage. The look on his face was priceless.

I jumped out and closed the garage door as the wailing siren started coming down the street. After the cop flew by, I opened the garage door, jumped back into my car, and backed out. He was standing in the same spot, wearing a flower-covered bathing suit, his mouth half open, and his hose rinsing the same spot. I slowly backed out, gave him a wink and half a wave, not a word spoken between us. I headed off in the other direction and Mike, who had sat quietly during all of this, was now busting a gut. It was a minor delay we hadn't expected, but we still made it home on time.

While I managed to skate to freedom that time, my Duster got me in quite a bit of trouble, too, because I didn't always get away. I thought it was fast and I wished it looked cool, but when the trunk finally rusted out bad enough for the gas tank to fall out on the ground, I sold it and bought a '65 Mustang. Cars were pretty cheap back then and the ones I was buying weren't exactly show cars.

When I got tired of that Mustang a year later, I bought a '69 Camaro SS with the 396 big block motor. It was an original SS with a four-speed transmission and I felt like I was moving up. Well, at least in cubic inches. This car wasn't going to win any beauty contests, either. At the time, I was a mechanic working at a Datsun dealer and I still

lived with my parents, which was about 10 miles from work. The body on my Camaro was pretty rough, but it ran great and my ride to work was all highway.

One particular morning, I had Mike with me. He also worked with me at the Datsun dealership and had become my best friend. Just as we were getting onto the entrance ramp, I saw two young boys with their thumbs out. They maybe looked 15, if that. Back then, and in our part of the country, hitchhiking was considered safe and done quite often. I was in a good mood, so I pulled over and they climbed into the back. I told them I was only going 10 miles and they said, "Cool man, anything helps."

As I got up to speed, I settled in the middle lane of the three-lane highway. Looking in my left rear view mirror, I noticed a pretty Corvette moving up behind me in the fast lane, but it was quite a ways back. I slowed down a little to let him catch up a bit. I wanted to get a better look. As it pulled alongside of us, I looked over and saw a beautiful '71 Corvette Mako Shark. Candy apple red paint with side pipes made it look hot and the honey sitting in the passenger seat looked even hotter. Mike and I gave them a thumbs up.

Did they smile? No! Did they wave? No! They both snubbed their noses up in the air and ignored us. Well, that just wasn't gonna do. I goosed it just enough to bounce my nose up a bit to see if he would bite. He did. With his side pipes right in my ear, I heard him hit it hard. I gave him a half a car before I down shifted and let it rip. I "walked" him by twenty car lengths before I backed off and coasted. I really wanted to humiliate him in front of his girl. I was quickly coming up on my exit, so I slowed way down. I wanted him to catch up. When he got along side of us, they were both giving us thumbs up with huge smiles on their face. As if on cue, Mike and I both flipped them off at the same time. I felt a lot better.

As I was getting off the highway, I thought I heard crying. Holy shit, I had completely forgotten about the two kids in the back seat. I pulled over on the exit ramp and let them out. You have never seen kids move like that. We laughed the whole rest of the way to work and the mornings events set the tone for the rest of the day.

Not too long later, I did a foolish thing. I traded the SS off. I loved the way that Camaro ran, but it was rough on the outside, with dents and dings, mismatched paint, and some temporary bodywork that was done shoddily. I knew nothing about bodywork or paint and I got tired of it looking like crap on the outside.

A friend down the street had bought a '71 Vega

hatchback. He had several other cars, so I didn't pay much attention to it at first. Then, one day while helping do some work to another car he had, I went into his large garage to grab a tool he needed. The Vega was sitting by itself in the corner under the lights and it stopped me in my tracks. It was flawless. It had new bright orange paint laid on a perfect body and was married to the ground with new five slot mags.

I didn't give the car much more thought however, because hey, it was a Vega. A while later as we began to finish what we were doing, I asked, "Hey Bill, what's up with the Vega in the garage?" He replied, "Oh, you haven't seen that one yet have you? Come on, let me show you". With all of his hot rods sitting around, I still didn't much care about a lowly Vega and wondered what it was doing in Bill's stable of cars. "Yeah," he said, "I paid a little too much for it, but I just had to have it".

"Why?" is all I thought. We walked over and he reached in and popped the hood release. I noticed a clean, stock interior. The car was in excellent shape, but I still wasn't that impressed. Then, he lifted the hood. It had a fully dressed 327 small block motor that was just as beautifully detailed as the rest of the car. You could have knocked me over with a feather. Other than under that hood, the entire car looked bone stock. Now I was impressed. "Wow, somebody did some nice work on this," I said.

"Yep, mildly built small block, a turbo 400, and you can't tell a thing from the outside" he bragged.

I fell in love on the spot… my soft spot for 'sleepers'. "You interested in selling it?" I asked.

"Nah, I bought it to keep", he quickly replied without thinking.

I said, "Bill, you already have enough toys, what does Vicki think about your latest purchase?"

157

"Don't ask" he replied.

Needless to say, we had to take it for a drive. It was a lot of fun seeing people's reaction to this thing lighting up the tires from a red light. It wasn't nearly as fast as my Camaro, but I liked it. "You sure you wouldn't sell it?"

"Nope, not interested," he said.

"What about a trade?" I said.

"A trade for what?"

"My Camaro".

I knew Bill loved my car the first time he rode in it. He already had a gorgeous '67 Camaro, but it didn't run like mine. Mine ran like a raped ape, but it definitely came up short in the looks department.

Long story short, Bill went for my offer and I drove the Vega home. It didn't take long to get in trouble with it, either. The very next day, I drove it to work and as I was leaving to go home, a few of the guys, including my buddy Mike, were standing outside. They yelled the usual stuff. "Where did you find that piece of shit?" "You sold your Camaro for that thing?" This was on the service side of the building, headed out to a four-lane road to go home.

The auto dealership where I worked, Busam Nissan, had just repaved the parking lot a few days earlier. There was a speed bump where they were standing, so as soon as my rear tires cleared the bump, I stopped. I stood on the brake a little bit and hit the gas. The tires spun effortlessly. I smoked those tires so bad that with the breeze behind me wafting smoke across the lot and down to the street, all four lanes of traffic on Kemper road came to a complete stop. The smoke was so thick that they couldn't see to drive through it. Keep in mind, I was on the side of the dealer showroom, which was a good forty yards from the street. I rolled off the speed bump, the guys each giving me a big thumbs up, and headed for home.

The next day, not long after I arrived, John Busam, the general manager, paged me on the intercom. "Jim, come to John's office." I didn't think much about it as I was up there a lot for work stuff anyway. "Do you like working here?" John asked.

"Sure I do John. Why?"

"That stunt you pulled last night when you were leaving was totally uncalled for."

"Sorry," I said.

"There were several people out on the lot that had to run inside the showroom because they couldn't breathe. Some of them ran in here choking." I had to keep myself from smiling, because John was really pissed. "I'm suspending you for three days so you can think about if you still want to work here".

"Is that like a three day vacation without pay?" (I always was a smart ass).

"Yep" he said.

"Ok, see you in three days," I said flippantly and left. I got high fives and handshakes from all the sales guys on my way back to the shop.

"That was the funniest thing I ever saw," said the sales manager. "I was out there too, and you couldn't see a damn thing. I had to feel my way back inside."

So, I got a mini vacation out of it.

The thrill eventually wore off and I sold the Vega to my best friend, Mike. On the first night Mike had the Vega, he was headed home on a curvy country road. He accidentally dropped a cigarette between his legs and as he frantically searched for it, he edged off the road and scraped a guardrail. Not so bad, right? Well not until the space in the rail grabbed the right front fender and peeled it off like a grape, then swung it around taking the entire front end and left fender, leaving them laying in several different places.

Mike was always like a brother to me. Sadly, life got in the way. He wound up in a different state, I was working and raising my family, and time created a void as it does so often. We lost touch in the mid-90s and recently, I have tried to find him. I'm sure it would be like no time had passed between us. But, with a name like Mike Smith, it's been the same as trying to find the proverbial needle in the haystack. Maybe he'll think of me and try to reach out. A Muckenfuhs might be easier to locate.

The Caddy and the Corvette

by Jon Schmidt

It was early evening, a Friday, in September of 1967. My best buddy, Jerry, and I were 16 and cruising the streets of Charlevoix, Michigan for chicks, adventure, or trouble in no particular order. We found all three.

We were in my '61 Ford Fairlane two-door post, a bright red chrome-laden machine complete with exhaust cut-outs that made it look and sound much meaner than it actually was. In reality, it boasted a small V8 2 barrel and Dual Range (2 speed) automatic transmission. My  father ran an auto body repair shop, so my cars tended to be shiny, but slow.

Jerry and I spotted two girls walking near downtown, one familiar and one unknown, both slim and attractive. I managed to find a parking spot a block or so up the street and we were leaning against my car nonchalantly as the girls approached.

Linda Walenski (or "Walnut" to her friends) was a curly-haired blonde that was a grade behind us at Charlevoix High. Her friend, Sherry Sheldon, was a new kid in town. Sherry was tall with shoulder length shiny brown hair and long legs in tight jeans. She said "Hi y'all" when Linda introduced us. It turned out that Sherry was a Kentucky girl and a military brat, uprooted to northern Michigan when her father was transferred to the local Air Force base.

Jerry preferred blondes and I liked brunettes, so the pairing up was painless. That evening was the first of many that he and I spent with that pair of beauties.

Sherry's dad was sent to Viet Nam, so I made myself indispensable to her mom and younger siblings. I baby-sat, shoveled snow, and ran errands; anything to ingratiate myself to the family. Captain Sheldon must have heard of my exploits because he included a "Thank you, Jon, for helping out while I'm gone" in one of his frequent letters. This gave me the courage to implement a plan that had been festering in the back of my mind.

Mrs. Sheldon's single stall garage housed a two year old AMC Rebel 6 cylinder automatic, brown inside and out, that looked like a military staff car. Boring! But next to the garage, exposed to the harsh northern Michigan climate, rested a 1956 Cadillac Coupe Deville. It was white with a black painted top, black interior with leopard print seat covers, and sombrero hubcaps. This was Captain Sheldon's civilian ride, and I felt duty bound to care for it.

This proud machine was parked facing the predominantly west wind coming off Lake Michigan, and by the first of the year, it was disappearing into a matching color snowbank. The time had come for action.

Sherry's mom was thrilled with my plan to get the Cadillac to my dad's shop and thaw it out over a weekend. Jerry and I moved the drifting snow encasing the car and popped the hood to attach jumper cables. The engine compartment was packed tight with snow, right up to the huge air cleaner housing two 4 barrel Rochesters. Surprise at the carburation was mingled with dismay at the snow encrusted big block. We obviously wouldn't be driving this beast as planned. But, I still wanted to get it to the shop.

Dad to the rescue!

My father loved old iron, especially large old iron, and he agreed to tow it to his shop with his 4 wheel drive truck. We managed to get the behemoth safely sheltered by late afternoon on a Saturday, and early Sunday morning found me in the shop cleaning plugs and drying wires. The battery was charged, and with a little gasoline down its throat, the beast roared.

I remember the adrenaline rush and the goose bumps on my arms as I sat behind the huge steering wheel and gunned the engine. All that raw power was mine!

I found a corner of the shop to park the Cadillac and spent what downtime I had touching up the small rust spots and polishing that old lacquer to a brilliant shine. I cleaned the interior, waxed the chrome, and even stripped the weather-checked roof and sprayed it with black enamel. I should mention that every so often, usually late at night, I'd take her out for a spin just to stretch her legs. I never tired of the way that Caddy would accelerate once it was moving. It lumbered off the line like the 5000 lb. machine that it was, but once those eight barrels kicked in ... hang on! I did, however, tire of putting gas in the hungry beast. Premium, no less.

Mrs. Sheldon had suggested that, as a reward for caring for the Caddy, Sherry and I should drive it to the upcoming Junior-Senior Prom. I felt honored and told her so.

On prom night, Jerry and Walnut were double dating with Sherry and I. Jerry met me at the shop and we took off in the Caddy to pick up the girls. We were 10 feet tall and bulletproof that night, two young studs in ill-fitting sports coats and ties, piloting what was sure to be the coolest ride at the dance. It was a fun evening with the girls, the Caddy, pictures, and lots of dancing.

After we dropped the girls off at their respective homes, Jerry and I were headed to the shop to park the Caddy for the night. There was a Sinclair gas station situated half way  up the hill on the four lane road leading south out of town. We had noticed, and commented on, a 1958 Corvette that often sat next to the building with its hood open. It was always there and what made it stand out was the color. It appeared to be pink. Jerry and I speculated that maybe the fluorescent lights lightened a faded red paint job or that maybe someone just mixed the paint wrong. It never entered our teenage minds that anyone would purposely paint a Corvette pink.

That night, as we started up the hill, the Corvette was just pulling out of the station and heading in the same direction. We were rolling along at maybe 40 or so when the 'Vette pulled up even in the next lane and started to pass. I glanced at Jerry, he nodded, and down went the gas pedal.

The Caddy hesitated momentarily, then unleashed everything it had as all of those barrels opened. I kept it floored as we crested the top of the hill and roared down the highway, too scared to look anywhere but straight ahead. The car jerked once as we sped past the Laundromat at 90 and I nearly lifted my foot until I realized we had just hit third gear.

I did let off at 100 and the old girl burbled happily through the factory duals as we slowed. Jerry was ecstatic, slapping me on the back, shouting that he had watched the 'Vette through the back glass, headlights bobbing as the driver shifted, trying to catch us.

A short ways out, we pulled into a Clark station. I said we needed gas but really, I was shaking too badly to drive. The pink Corvette pulled in and a young man a few years older than us walked up smiling with his hand out. Turns out he was in the Air Force, stationed at the local base, and worked on the 'Vette at the Sinclair station every chance he had. The Corvette had a lot of miles on it and was pink when he bought it. He was slowly restoring it as time and money allowed.

We peered under each other's hoods and talked cars for a while, but I needed to get the car put away at the shop. I told him about my father's business and he agreed to come see us when he was ready for paint.

A few months later, the Corvette disappeared from the station. I cruised past the base a couple of times, but never saw it again. I was sure that the military had deployed its owner to another location and I hoped it wasn't Southeast Asia.

I will never forget the adventure of the Caddy and the Corvette.

When Jerry and I went looking for girls, adventure, and trouble that night in September of 1967, we were successful. Linda and Sherry were our girlfriends throughout our senior year of high school. Sadly, Sherry and her family moved back to Kentucky and our long distance relationship soon faded.

Walnut just moved on and the '61 Ford got swapped for the next car in a succession of many. It's like the old saying goes. Cars and girls... you can't keep them all.

Sprinting Along

by Larry Carnes

During the 70's and 80's, my Dad and I restored cars. The restorations, while good, were not concourse quality by any means, though we did have a nice collection of trophies for our efforts. What we really had was a little business. We would find a classic car to fix up, purposely put it in a show to get a trophy, and then sell it. Much like the various car 'flip' shows seen on television today!

For a teenage kid, this was heaven. I learned a lot about cars and the main benefit was that I could drive any car I wanted. Dad knew that I was obsessed with keeping a car polished and running well, so he figured my driving a car was like a rolling advertisement.

One year, we found a 1966 Mustang "Sprint", which was supposedly a 'special edition' Mustang. The reality was that Ford had a shortage of 289cid V8s, so they threw a 200cid straight 6 in some Mustangs with a chrome air cleaner that said "Sprint" and called it an option package.

So, we purchased the car and began the process of restoring it. I asked to drive it because I knew a few young ladies who liked Mustangs and had always liked them myself. My father agreed as long as I did not "race" the Mustang. For some reason, he felt I raced the cars which was untrue. I worked so hard on them that the last thing I wanted to do was damage one!

In any event, I began driving the Sprint to college and would fix the various things I found wrong, like loose steering or catchy brakes. I tuned the engine until it purred. One day, I stopped at a local mall to purchase a shirt and began leaving in the normal fashion. I backed the Mustang out of the parking spot, put it in drive, and suddenly the accelerator pedal leaped to the floor as if it had been shoved down hard, the light Mustang screeching its tires down the parking lot at high speed.

Frantically, I tried to pull the pedal up with the toe of my foot to no avail. I tried hard not to panic, but I was running out of parking lot and headed for the main road. I put both feet on the brake but still couldn't stop, so I turned the car off and managed to slow it down. I coasted to an empty part of the parking lot and looked under the hood and found nothing out of the ordinary.

I cranked the car and it idled perfectly. I revved the motor a few times and found no problem. Putting the car in reverse caused no problem, either, so I dropped it into "D" and the accelerator pedal shot to the floor and the Mustang took off again! This time I slid the car in neutral and immediately the accelerator popped up.

So, I drove the car home by alternately putting the car in Drive, building up speed and then sliding it into neutral and coasting. When I arrived home, I popped the hood to examine the motor and had no sooner done so when my father arrived home and asked "What's wrong with the Sprint?"

When I told him my story he immediately began shaking his head and said "You just don't know how to drive this car!" I was momentarily speechless, but finally said "What do you mean? Is this car any different than the dozen or so I've driven before?" As I was saying this, he slammed the hood down and hopped in the driver's seat and cranked the car and said "See! This car runs perfectly!" I replied, "It only happens when you put it in gear!" Before I could explain further, he put it in Reverse and backed out the driveway and turned the car to point down the road. "See! There's nothing wrong with this car! You just can't drive!"

I grinned and said "Put it in Drive!" Again, my father started berating me, but as he dropped it into Drive, the little Mustang lit up a tire and shot down the street with my father yelling "WHOA! WHOA! WHOA!" at the top of his voice.

I fell to the ground doubled over in laughter as he shot over a hill. A few moments later he came back driving in Reverse. "You were right! This car is dangerous!" he said, as he stepped out. After he changed clothes, we went over the car and found that the left motor mount had broken and when the car was put into Drive, the engine would twist, pulling on the accelerator cable, causing more gas to be delivered to the engine, which meant more torque and more twisting until the pedal was floored.

My dad and I had many other funny adventures during the 25 years we worked on cars together, along with many arguments, but I wouldn't trade those years for anything.

The Ford in My Future

by Jon Schmidt

We were both 15 and too young to drive, but both interested in all things automotive. I'm sure that shared interest was what sparked the initial attraction between Mary Ann Gulliver and me about a year before.

Together, we impatiently awaited the arrival of each new issue of *Hot Rod Magazine*, *Popular Hot Rodding*, and the little pages of *Car Craft* and *Custom Rodder* at the local newsstand. We would dispute the pros and cons of each showcased car, voicing what we'd like to change to make each one our very own. I leaned toward chrome and pinstripes while Mary Ann dreamed of flashy two-tone paint jobs. In retrospect, I worked after school and weekends at my father's  auto body repair and paint shop, and perhaps this added to my personal allure.

Sometime during the winter of 1965, Mary Ann and I discovered that maybe there was more to our relationship than a shared love of automobiles. I suddenly saw her in a new light, less as a fellow car maven and more as a fair maiden. I started bathing more, dressing better, and even added English Leather cologne to my list of toiletries.

Mary Ann eventually noticed the changes. She laughed out loud at her discovery and wanted to know who I had a crush on. I gave her my best love-sick puppy dog look designed to melt female hearts of all types and persuasions. She said "Eeeww! You look like you have to fart! Go outside!"

Soon, however, subtle changes in our relationship pointed toward a budding romance. Mary Ann shed her perpetual ponytail in favor of permed curly hair. She showed up at my house one day with the latest *Rod and Custom* wearing a knee length jumper and nylon stockings. I couldn't take my eyes off her legs. She had legs!

Our romance progressed slowly as young loves tend to do. Our list of "firsts" grew as winter progressed: first real date, first time holding hands, first slow dance, and first kiss. I was in love with a fellow car nut and life couldn't get any better.

Well, except for one thing. There was one more first for us and it was the big one. We talked about being in love and about commitment and about consummating our relationship. We agreed to the act, but also agreed that it had to be at a special time and place.

Mary Ann picked the date of one year exactly since we first shared a car magazine downtown at the newsstand. That had been a Thursday afternoon in early March, a Friday this year, just two weeks away. Now, the question was where?

There are not a lot of places in small town northern Michigan where two young lovers can find some privacy, especially when they are pedestrians. Careful questioning revealed that neither set of parents had plans for that evening. Too cold for outside. We lacked the courage to rent a motel room in our town and lacked transportation to another town. What to do?

The answer came to me early one morning as I showered before school. Dad's body shop! It was warm and within walking distance and full of cars with back seats. We could have our pick and I had a key!

Mary Ann actually liked the idea. We loved cars and each other. It seemed the perfect place to share that love.

Our special Friday finally arrived. I went to work at the shop after school, my mind anywhere but on the task at hand. I kept picturing Mary Ann in various vehicles in various stages of undress. Could time pass any slower?

Around 5 p.m. Dad announced that he was going out to write an estimate and then going home. He instructed me to paint the door jambs and under the hood and trunk lid on the car in the spray booth. Then, noticing the blank look on my face, he told me again because I was lost in a fog of desire.

I opened the door to the booth and gazed at a 1959 Ford sedan, gray interior, primer and white body, ready for a complete paint job. All of the windows were masked off, so I had to open a door to look at the back seat. Bingo! We have a winner, folks! The spacious seat and extra privacy of the paint booth were perfect for that night's adventure.

I loaded white lacquer in the spray gun and carefully shot around the doors, hood, and deck lid. We used lacquer for this step back then because it sprayed at lower pressure and dried quickly. Complete body paint jobs were usually done using enamel paint that dried shiny but took overnight to dry.

I unhooked the battery and left the hood and trunk open. The doors I shut just enough to catch but not all the way. I cleaned the spray gun, locked up, and ran home to dinner.

Mary Ann was a vision of loveliness that evening when I arrived at her house to escort her to a high school basketball "away" game. We were supposed to catch a spectator bus at the school, which would return around 10 p.m. Instead, we walked through a light snow to the shop.

We made our way in the dark back to the Ford in the paint booth and then crawled into the back seat, fully clothed and still wearing coats and boots. I carefully shut the car door. Alone at last with at least two hours to spend any way we wanted.

It was dark and a bit cold and there wasn't much room to maneuver in our bulky coats. We kissed, I unbuttoned and removed her coat, then mine, and laid them on the rear floor. Boots joined the pile. Buttons were undone, zippers came open, and the temperature rose dramatically. I had just undone Mary Ann's bra when the booth lights came on.

Mary Ann took a breath to scream, but I covered her mouth with my hand, shaking my head frantically. We sat frozen in a pile of discarded clothing, barely breathing, wide-eyed and scared. The air compressor turned on with a loud clunk, then the overspray fans in the spray booth came alive, adding to the din.

Omigod! Dad had returned to paint the Ford! He often sprayed after hours to avoid dust, phone calls, and customers. Had he told me that afternoon that he was coming back to work? I was so distracted that day, dreaming of the evening to come, I could have easily missed that announcement.

We heard Dad enter the booth and blow the dust off the car, then he slammed the hood and trunk. The driver's door started to open and I thought I'd faint, but he just clunked it all the way closed. Ditto the other doors. No interior lights came on because the battery was disconnected to keep them off while the door jambs dried. I was thankful that I had remembered that detail earlier in the day.

The paint job progressed, taking much longer than I thought it should, and there we sat, too afraid to move throughout the procedure. 90 minutes and 3 coats later the compressor clicked off, the fans stopped, and the booth lights went off. Soon, we heard the outside door slam shut.

We each let loose with long sighs of relief. As my eyes adjusted to the lack of light, I gazed at this beautiful nymph before me and felt a rush of desire. I touched her where bra met breast. She pushed me away with both hands.

"Are you nuts?" she hissed. "After all that, you still want to do it?"

Well … yeah.

But, we didn't. Instead we dressed as best we could and carefully extracted ourselves from the freshly painted car. We ran to school and managed to get the details of the game from some lingering teens. Parents always asked "How was the game?" and we needed to be prepared.

I walked Mary Ann home and received a quick kiss before she ran inside. My folks were both up when I came into our house. They asked about the game and I regurgitated the details, hoping they were correct.

I was headed upstairs to bed when Dad asked the question. "Hey, Jonnie, you weren't in the shop tonight, were you?"

I stopped and slowly turned around. He stood at the base of the stairs, squinting into the overhead light. I'm sure my face was red, but the light was behind me masking my features.

"I went down after supper to paint," he continued, "and there were wet footprints by the door. Looked like someone, or maybe two someone's, came in and stomped the snow off their shoes. But you were at the game, right?"

"And a great game it was!" I replied. "You should have seen our defense. Unbelievable! Good night." I hurried to bed, but didn't sleep for quite some time.

Dad and I went to work on Saturday morning as usual. I was peeling the masking paper off the freshly painted Ford when he came into the booth.

"This one is heading for the Ford dealer's used car lot," he said. "A few years old, but lower mileage and in great  shape, just scratched up, easier to paint the whole thing than try to spot it. Anyway, look it over and see if you like it. Maybe we can make a deal with them. This would make a good car for you."

I stood there looking at him, not knowing what to say. He smiled and said "Think about it. This is a really clean car. Those seats look like they've never been sat on … especially in back."

I ended up buying that 1959 Ford and painting it two-tone copper and white per Mary Ann's suggestion. Any further adventures we may have had involving the car shall remain unrecorded.

My father lived for another thirty two years and never admitted that he knew we were in the car that night.

Forgotten Pencil Drawing

by Lloyd (Bud) Norton

Back in 2007 when my wife, Marilyn, and I were relatively new to the car show scene, we took "Little Lulu", our '40 Chevrolet business coupe, to the Little Creek Casino near Shelton, WA for the "Cool Creek Nites Car Show." We went the day before the show with a small group of car people that we hung out at car shows with and spent the night at the casino.

Now, even though this was at the end of August, we woke up the next morning to an overcast sky. The weather got progressively worse during the day and at around 3:00 PM we felt the first sprinkles. Not wanting to get caught in an outright rainstorm 80 miles from our home in North Tacoma, we started packing up our stuff to make a quick getaway.

We made some hurried goodbyes and pulled onto Hwy 101 heading east back toward Olympia. While approaching the turnoff from Hwy 101 to Northbound I-5, we got a call on our cell phone. It was one of our friends from the car show. Apparently, a group of wives who weren't all that excited about car shows was returning from a day of shopping in Olympia when they saw "Little Lulu" going in the other direction.

They noticed something odd stuck to the front of our car. So, one of the ladies called her husband, who in turn called us. Not knowing what they were talking about, we pulled over to the side of the freeway as soon as we were safely able to. I got out of the car and walked around to the front where "Lo and Behold" there it was.

We had forgotten to pack up part of our display. It was an 11" X 14", framed under glass, pencil sketch of an aban-  doned 1940 Chev Coupe in the weeds. It was nestled between the bumper and the front fender and hadn't moved an inch. It had just travelled 18 miles in that position without any scratches in the picture frame or car paint or any broken glass.

I would say that that was a real tribute to our Heidts Mustang II Front Independent Suspension, wouldn't you?

From a Rat to a King

by David Dickinson

In 1971, I was a fresh faced kid in the USN. I had been assigned to the USS England DLG22, which was just finishing a yard period at the shipyard in Bath, Maine. In fact, the ship had been decommissioned and been completely overhauled. Once the ship was finished, it was re-commissioned and I was what they called a "plank owner", part of the initial crew on a new ship.

When we left the shipyard on our shakedown cruise, many interesting locales were on the list of stops prior to settling into the base at Long Beach, California. The entire east coast and much of the west coast of the north and south Americas was navigated with stops in Norfolk, Virginia; Guantanamo Bay, Cuba; Rio de Janeiro, Brazil; the Panama Canal Zone and Panama City, Panama and finally Acapulco, Mexico. Pulling into Long Beach was a bit of a letdown after that, I can assure you.

Once settled into daily activities in Long Beach, we were not scheduled to do too much traveling for quite some time and so, I set about trying to position myself into my new environment as more than just a young sailor. I got an apartment and filled it with cheap furnishings and kitchenware from the local second hand store and determined I didn't want to ride a bus anymore then than I did in high school. So, I went looking for wheels.

I can't say that up to that point I had been a fan of Corvairs, having received my first ticket and losing my license in one during a "contest of speed" during my junior year of high school. The car belonged to a couple of sisters I knew and it was their entire fault. Honest! The long and short of it is that I was chauffeuring them around in it one

night and they wanted me to chase a friend in a hot rod Ford. He kept going faster and they kept egging me on to catch up. Well, we both got pulled over and I lost what the judge assumed was a race and my license to boot! Some race!

So, when I was looking for a car in Long beach, Chevy's possibly least finest wasn't my first choice, but it was affordable and I was the almost proud owner of a 1960 Corvair. Once I put new brakes on it and cleaned it up, I actually enjoyed driving it. It was kind of a rat, as far as I was concerned, but I spent lots of hours cruising up and down I-5 and I-405 in SoCal, making new friends and hauling around those I already knew … that didn't have cars.

After a couple of months of coming and going from my apartment to the Naval base, my landlord approached me, telling me how cool he thought the Corvair was and how he missed one that he had driven in years past. Finally, he got around to telling me what was really on his mind. He wanted the car. I told him I really didn't have any interest in selling it just to begin a search for another car. Thanks, but no thanks.

He wasn't done propositioning me, however, and had a real Ace up his sleeve. He told me "I've got a car that I'd trade you straight across for, if you want." I wasn't real excited, but played along. "Come with me", he said. So, having a few minutes and a bit of curiosity, I followed him around back to his garage. Sitting there, almost as pretty as the day it rolled off the showroom floor, was a 1959 Chevrolet Impala Sport Coupe. I was a little surprised, to say the least.

"What's the deal?" I asked. "Does it run?"

"It runs great, but I bought it to surprise my wife and she hates it. She says it looks like it's ready to flap its rear wings and leave the ground!" was his muted reply. I could tell he wasn't happy with her, but wanted to keep her happy.

Trying to contain myself, I asked if it needed anything mechanical. I didn't have the money to put another set of brakes on a car or anything else for that matter. He assured me that the car was in great shape and very roadworthy, but he had his truck and she wouldn't drive it, either. He did reveal that she continually brought up the little Corvair that the guy in Apt 6 came and went in. That would be me and my little white baby that I was about to parlay into a real car.

After completing the trade, and having more room for passengers, I was really popular among the other guys on my ship. I never minded the company and there were always lots of adventures, not to mention the endless source of gas money that was being thrown my way. If a buddy wanted to go north to see his girl, and introduce me to her girlfriend, I had wheels and he had gas money. It worked out really well for me. I was King of the Road!

It really turned out to be a great road car with its 348 cubic inch V8 and automatic transmission. In the time that I owned that car, I do not remember ever having to spend any money on repairs. It would jump on the freeway and accelerate like it had been launched from a cannon. At that point, it was one of the nicest, most powerful cars I had ever owned. When I think back to all of the cars I say I wish I still had, this is the one that comes to mind first. Of course, I say that about each one as I relate their particular stories.

I remember vividly, one night on my way back to Long Beach from a special young lady's home in Sherman Oaks, that I was tired and in a hurry. The weekend fun was over and I needed to get some rest and be ready for the week. It was late and the traffic wasn't too heavy coming south on I-405. I was going about 85 miles per hour and moving in and out of traffic, changing lanes to keep my speed.

The long arm of the law came swooping down on me in the form of red lights in my rear view mirror. Damn, busted again! I pulled over and removed my license from my wallet and the registration from the glove box, anticipating a ticket and a serious lecture from California's finest. The young CHP officer approached the car and asked me why I was in such a hurry.

"Just trying to get back to my ship, Officer" was my reply.

"Well, do you know why I pulled you over?" he teased.

"Speeding?" was my reply without thinking.

"Yes, but I want to compliment you, as well!" He surprised me with that. "You were going too fast, but I appreciate that you were also being very cautious and signaling your every move." Boy was I glad to have good turn signals and the common sense to use them.

"Look", he says, "if you'll promise to slow it down and get back to your ship safely, I'll let this go with a verbal and you can be on your way. I was in the Navy myself and had an officer do the same for me one night. Just slow it down, OK?"

Completely surprised at his graciousness, I acknowledged his warning and his generosity. I drove the speed limit the rest of the way home, grateful that I didn't have to pay for a ticket or have a ticket on my record and deal with the fallout, including higher insurance premiums. By the way, I was one of the guys insured by Geico way back then when it was called Government Employees Insurance Company and you had to be a government employee to qualify. The rates were cheaper for military, but you had to keep a good driving record.

The party with the '59 Impala ended when my ship was scheduled to depart on a Westpac tour with lots of cool destinations, like Midway Island, Japan, Thailand, Singapore, Hong Kong and more... oh, and one that was not so exciting; the Gulf of Tonkin.

So, the '59 Impala was sold, we did our tour of duty, and upon return to the States I settled into another car and other adventures. Its funny how each car comes with its own set of adventures, isn't?

Return of the '32

by Ron Limbrick

There are only a few personal firsts that really stick out in a guy's mind. I'm sure we all can think of at least two. My first car has to rank right up there very close to the top of my list and I would bet that you feel the same about your first car. Let me tell you about my memories of my first … car that is.

It was early May of 1955 and spring was just beginning on the north shore of Lake Superior, which meant that getting around and exploring car lots on your bicycle was the perfect thing to do when you are one month away from your all-important 16th birthday.

I can remember rolling past Dominion Motors used car lot, which was just down the street from my home in Fort William, Ontario, where something caught my eye sitting in the back row. I immediately recognized what I saw and made a beeline to the back of the lot. What was sitting before me was what all of the car magazines were full of in 1955, a 1932 Ford 5 window coupe. Wow! This is what they were talking about!

Fort William, now called Thunder Bay, is a world away from San Diego geographically, but for that instance, they were one and the same. My enthusiasm and inexperience overlooked the many imperfections and all I saw was the beauty in black. I made my way to the sales office to find out what the asking price was for her. After a quick search, I found Mr. Winters (I'm positive that was his name) and he told me that "the fine little car was $75." No time to bargain, I had to get back home to tell my Dad about it as fast as I could. It's not every day you find a '32 coupe for sale for $75.

I had all the finances worked out in my head by the time I burst through the front door. I could sell my outboard motor that wasn't  needed anymore. Someone had stolen the boat that my Dad and I had built the year before. I could find a job to pay for the balance. It was all going to work out. I just knew it was.

Well, I must have caught my Mom and Dad on a really good day as the coupe was in our yard by nightfall. I was one very lucky 15 year old, wouldn't you say?

I remember getting my beginner's permit on my 16th birthday and driving My '32 "B" with its new brushed red paint job to get my driver's license the very next day. The tester asked me how many miles I had driven with the beginner's permit to which I responded, "about 15." He said, "We had better make that 150."

He then directed me to drive him around the block, then drop him off at the front door of the Vehicle License Office, where he said, "You are doing just fine. Go and park it and come in and get your license."

Yahoo! As you might expect, I had a great summer learning about cars and driving. However, I was still way too short to pick up chicks. Looking back on it all now, It would have been great to have had an older brother that could have tutored me in Hot Rod 101, as I think I had the" Jughead Jalopy" mentality back in those days. With the proper role model looking over my shoulder, I'm sure I could have done a better job. Oh, well.

I traded the '32 in on a '40 Ford coupe the next spring and while the '40 was cool, I missed the '32 almost right  away. Over the many years that passed, I kept hearing reports that my '32 was still in town but I could never verify that until very recently when a friend of a friend gave me a name and phone number that might lead me somewhere. Sure enough, it did.

I called the phone number and told the lady that answered who I was and why I was calling. She was pleasant and told me what she knew of the car and its history over the last fifty some years since I had traded it off. At this point, it was sitting in her garage and had been for many years. I asked if she would be interested in selling the car and she responded with those dreaded words, "The car is not for sale." So, I asked if I could come by and take look and maybe some pictures.

She agreed and I went over as soon as I could gather my wits and my camera. We had a pleasant time chatting and wandering around the '32, which had been off the road for many years. It had a thick layer of dirt, flat tires, and, of course, didn't run. To my eyes, she was beautiful.

As I left, holding back tears, I let the lady know that I would like to have the '32 back someday, should she decide to sell. I could only hope she would call.

Five years later, about the time I had figured she had probably sold the car to someone else and given up hopes of the '32 returning to me, I got unexpected news. One day after coming home from having coffee with some friends, my wife, Joan, said, "You had better listen to the phone messages", which I did. To my surprise, there was a message from the lady who owned the '32 that had let me take the pictures of it those five long years ago. She remembered that I left her with "if you ever want to sell it, please call me as that car sure does mean a lot to me." She told me that she had been saving it for her son, but tragically, he had passed away. She asked if I was still interested.

A few days passed while she had someone estimate for her what they thought was a fair price and she contacted me again. Naturally, I accepted and now my first car will be my last. After selling it once, I cannot fathom selling it again.

I mentioned that if I had an older brother to guide me in Hot Rod 101, I wouldn't have had the Jug Head mentality that I had when I first bought the car at 15. With the '32 returning home after all of these years, I just realized that I am now that "older brother".

A Wonderful Day

by Will and Rhonda Johnson

Have you ever have one of those days when everything just goes right? Well, they happen and I'm here to say one just happened to me. It all started the night before. I had one of those nights when I slept like a baby. You know; the kind of sleep you have when nothing wakes you and you get up feeling very rested and full of energy. Yeah, it was kinda like that.

I think that life is a series of little things we do daily to make our life better for tomorrow. Or as I like to put it... setting yourself up for something bigger and better. I truly believe that the way we treat each and every one in our lives is a reflection of good things to be returned to us on a future date.

Case in point: recently I was in the doctor's office getting some lab work done and the technician was drawing a sample of my blood for some sort of analysis. I was sitting in the lab chair as the lab tech worked on my outstretched arm. He was trying to make me feel somewhat comfortable with small talk as he applied his skilled technique of jabbing skin and expressing his firm, but coarse, bedside manner. About this time another patient came in and sat on the bench in the hallway to await his destiny with a similar fate as mine; lab work that is. As patients, simply mutual customers of the lab, we have no idea what's wrong with each other and if our two alleged problems are even remotely similar. Still, you do wonder.

As I was finishing up and removing myself from the chair of submission and pain, allowing for my fellow patient to be tortured, I couldn't help but notice he was wearing a shirt with an Oldsmobile car on it. I commented on the shirt and told him about having an engine for such a car and that I was in the process of hunting for a tri power set up for it. I said this in passing, not meaning too much other than I was aware that this option was available back in 1957 on the J-2 models and finding one would be quite a treasure, being that they are extremely rare.

Now, to my surprise the man replied that he had one and would gladly give it to me. WOW! I mean, Wow! Can I really believe what I have just heard with my own two ears? I about broke my arm getting my wallet out to find a card with my name on it so I could leave him my phone number. I had to at least see such a thing and secretly thought that maybe he only wanted to sell it and was probably not all that generous. But still, he did say "give", and I know this is the part where I'm supposed to say I will buy it from him and what will he take in hard cash for it, but I only had a little money available to spend at the time and just figured I'd better keep quiet.

After all, it was a want and not a need. I introduced myself and gave my newfound car buddy a card with my phone number on it so he could contact me. I then departed, as all my doctor visit was used up. I made sure I said a fond fair well to all and beat it.

Fast-forward two months. I never saw or heard a peep from the man I had the conversation with at my last visit to the lab in the doctor's office and, knowing that talk is sometimes very cheap among some hot rodders and car people, I just figured he thought better of his generous offer and would most likely avoid me like the plague.

Amazingly, when the phone rang last night I was

surprised and delighted to hear the voice of the Oldsmobile man; a true man among men, a true prince of a person that I personally can never say enough good things about. He said, "I have been hauling this part around in my car for over a month now. I want to give it to you, like I had said, and need to know where I can meet with you."

"Well sir, I have breakfast each morning at a small restaurant with some old car guys. If you want I can meet you there and buy you breakfast", I offered.

"That sounds good. I'll see you there at eight thirty."

"That will be fine. I'm driving a small green Ford Escort."

"That's kinda funny, 'cause I'm driving one also, only in red", he replies.

Well, remember at the beginning of this story, I was talking about a wonderful day when everything goes perfect? Well, this is the start of that day.

I met Mr. Rick Block today and he joined me for coffee at the small restaurant that I frequent with my car friends. He had, true to his word, brought the tri-power manifold  along and we loaded it into my car before entering the restaurant.

I introduced him to my friends and had a small, modest breakfast. I bought his coffee and had offered to buy him breakfast. He said "No, but thanks just the same." We talked about old hot rods and all of my old car buddies enjoyed his company.

He told us of some of the cars he had and that made us all drool. I stayed as long as time would permit me, but the day was moving forward and having other obligations to take care of and places to go, said my good byes.

I can hardly believe all this good fortune happening to me of all people. Life is good!

The morning continued and I spent most of it with my son, both of us trying to make some much-needed extra cash. We are helping a friend of mine clean up his place, sorting and removing a lot of old iron and metals for the recyclers. I figure, with the price of gas these days, we will hardly make anything on the scrap, but what the heck, we weren't doing much anyway and any money is good money.

We took our load in, weighed it, and got paid. The workers at the recycle company have seen us a little more often lately. I have had to sell a few things in order to do some of the projects I have lined up and they treat us very generously. The funds are split between the three of us, and after the gas expense is deducted, we have all done pretty well.

This is the first day of the summer and it is very warm and pleasant. I return home and get ready for a get together with some old car friends later that day. As my wife and valued co-pilot, Rhonda, and I drive out of town in our '57 Thunderbird convertible with its top down, the wind is warm and I turn up some old music. It's loud enough to overcome the engine and road noise and we sing along all the way to our destination. We have a great time at the gathering and, once again, it's time to head back home, leaving the top down and our sweatshirts on. It's a lot cooler now, but at about sixty miles an hour with the wind, music, and tires humming ... life is good.

It is a perfect day in my life and as I purr down the road, I secretly give thanks to a higher power for an absolutely wonderful day.

Pizza Sauce & 30W Oil

by Lance Lambert

My first experiences working on cars were during my years of being a pest while my big brother Jay was working on his 1933 Buick, 1939 and 1948 Fords, and 1949 Chevrolet. He would give me some simple job, with the results usually leaving me either burned or bleeding. With this confidence building training I became ready for my own car.

My first car was a 1948 Chevrolet Fleetline (the 24 hour ownership of a 1949 Dodge doesn't count). After one day  of owning it, I'd gotten my first ticket and after one week of driving, I'd blown up the motor. The next several weeks were spent sitting in the car and pretending that it still ran. I had purchased the car to drive, not use as a playhouse, so something had to be done.

Jay had made me realize one major thing about working on cars; I didn't enjoy it. Sure, I could hang a muffler; change the oil, and other such "no brainers." But I saw the real mechanical work as both a mystery and an unappealing chore.

So, there I sat in my Chev pretending to be cruising past my high school and enjoying the admiring glances of my classmates. In reality the only people that saw me were the neighbors who likely wondered why the car and its young occupant just sat there.

It was time for action.

My friend Greg, a real mechanic, was replacing the original six cylinder engine in his 1940 Chevrolet coupe with a Chev 283 V8. What was he going to do with that now surplus six cylinder engine? He answered that question by selling it to me for a price that was very easy for him to "stomach." That left me with the chore of putting it into my Fleetline.

Another question was how could I explain to friends at the local hangouts that I had replaced my '48 engine with the engine from a '40 Chev? That seemed to be going backwards, against all that was held holy by any young hot rodder.

I had a friend that removed the V8 engine from his '55 Ford and replaced it with a six cylinder engine out of a school bus. He was going to be the only guy on the planet that would be lower in the hot rodder pecking order than me.

I came up with an answer! I told everyone that my "new" motor was out of a '49 Chevrolet. That would be acceptable by our stringent standards, so the problem was solved. The fact that all of our mutual friends knew that the motor from Greg's car was being transplanted into my car didn't seem to enter my mind. Research shows that a 16-year-old brain is not fully formed. I was proof of that theory.

Now, the big problem was how I would join Greg's old engine and my Chev body in holy matrimony? It was time for me to reach deep into my bag of tricks and solve the problem. I had a secret weapon - a weapon that none of my non-mechanically challenged buddies could resist. I had at my disposal a weapon that was so powerful that it was second only to the allure of attention from pubescent females. I had pizza!

I had been working at the local pizza restaurant for several months, and most of the local teenagers were crazy about pizza. During my short tenure, the manager and I had come to an agreement. He was a hardcore alcoholic who wanted to spend as much time as possible across the street at the local tavern. I worked three weekday evenings and Saturdays. During that time he would cross the street for a refueling that would take the entire evening, leaving me in charge of running the joint. He wouldn't even return to close the restaurant. He gave me the title of assistant manager, but my wage remained at $1.25 per hour. I got the title so that the staff would do what this 16-year-old kid told them to do.

But here was the real payoff: he always "looked the other way" when it came to my form of food distribution. I traded pizza for beer. I traded pizza for car parts. I traded pizza for the use of the hoist and tools at the local Union 76 gas station where a friend worked. I fed pizza to a destitute 16-year-old friend who lived on his own. I brought pizza home to my family. And I traded Greg a pizza for his old engine. This monetary system worked great and it also resulted in that little six-cylinder engine being installed in my Chev and a pepperoni pizza being installed in Greg's stomach.

Yes, it was stealing from the company and, looking back, I feel a bit guilty about it. I convinced myself at the time that, given all of the circumstances, it was an acceptable way to make up for my lack of a raise for running the place, and also for not "ratting out" my boss.

I told my buddies Greg, Doug, Bob, and Darrol that they could have as much free pizza as they wanted, whenever they wanted it, if they would install Greg's surplus engine in my car and get it running properly. I said that I would help, but it was up to them to do the majority of the real work. What would have likely taken me weeks to do took them only one weekend to complete.

I have proof that I actually got my hands dirty while helping with the installation. My mother took a picture of us while we were doing the transplant. I was under the car at the time and gave her a smile. Fortunately, she did not take a photo at other times when I fell asleep under the car. Not just relaxing; I was sound asleep. The rest of the group didn't even notice and they did an excellent job of doing my work for me. By the end of the weekend the car ran great and I had gotten some much-needed sleep.

Now it was time for me to "pay" my mechanics. Those guys could put away pizza and they were "paid" handsomely for their time and talents. I worked at the restaurant for about 18 months and during that time they came in frequently to receive their wages.

The whole pizza thing was just getting started in Tacoma in 1963 and where I worked was one of the first pizza parlors in town. It was always very busy and crowded with my friends. A few of these friends had 30-weight oil and pizza sauce on their hands. That's OK, because they didn't need to reach into their pockets for money.

Heroes, Promises, and Survivors

by Erich Bailey

My love of American cars began in 1961 at the age of 15. I was a German citizen, and after seven long years living in an orphanage, my brother and I were reunited with our mother, younger two sisters, and brother. My new stepfather, Edward H. Bailey, a US Army WWII veteran stationed at Schweinfurt, Germany was brave enough to adopt all five of us and was prepared to take us back to the USA. He was my new hero and as a bonus, he had an awesome '55 Chevrolet station wagon. It was the first American car I ever rode in and was part of my becoming a lover of old American cars. My mother named it "Leisel" which, in German, means "God's promise"…a fitting name for what was part of a new beginning for all of us.

When my stepfather was transferred to Fort Ord, California, "Liesel" was loaded on the ship USS Upshur, along with all seven of us, and we made our way to New York City. We drove our Chevrolet across the USA to California and what a great trip that was as we watched another of God's Promises roll out before us,  mile after mile. I was proud to be an American.

Sometime in 1963, I was able to land a part-time job at $1.25 per hour. Eventually, I saved enough money to buy my first car. It was a '57 Chevrolet Bel Air and I paid

$900 for it with the help of my parents. I would take my girlfriend to the local drive-in movie or sometimes cruise up and down Alvarado Street in Monterey on weekend evenings. We often drove the Bel Air to Big Sur and Pacific Grove's Lovers Point.

When I had surgery on my shoulder and could only use one arm to drive, I attached a "Suicide Knob" to the steering wheel and I got around just fine in spite of my temporary disability. Those were the days!

Sadly, I did some really dumb things to that poor car, like removing the gold V8 emblems, plugging up, and painting over the holes. Once, I offered to give a push to my friend's Ford when he couldn't start it. That event broke the beautiful front grill to pieces, leaving a large gaping black hole in front of the radiator.

A '61 Corvair Monza caught my eye one day in 1964 and the final insult to the beautiful Bel Air was to trade

it in. Corvairs were fun little cars, but the fun was short lived because I knew I would soon be drafted into the Army. It was the Viet Nam war era and instead of waiting to be drafted, I decided to join the Air Force in 1965. So, I had to give up the Corvair.

The Air Force, Viet Nam, and marriage to that same girl I cruised with in my '57 Chevy Bel Air with the suicide knob, along with three kids, including surprise twin girls, were my priority the next years. My cars, mostly Chevrolets, were just basic necessities for the family and work. We shipped our family car, a giant Chevrolet Kingswood station wagon, to Chitose AB, Hokkaido, Japan, where I was stationed for two years. It was lots of fun navigating those narrow streets there in that giant American station wagon!

In 1967, at the age of 60, my father in law, Tom Di Mercurio, another one of my heroes, bought a Marina blue '67 Chevrolet Impala Sport coupe right off the showroom floor from Roller Chevrolet in Monterey, California. He always wanted a car like that and after working hard all his life and raising four daughters, he finally was able to get it for $3600, a lot of money to him back then. He would jokingly say one thing he liked about that car is he could easily carry an eight foot 2x4 home from the lumberyard in it with only a short part of it sticking out the window. I fell in love with that car from the first moment that I saw it. While he owned it, it never left the state of California and he put less than 35,000 miles on it before he passed away in 1985.

The car survived a teenage grandson, who did some tinkering to it for a couple of years, before my wife and I took ownership in 1987 and in turn gave it to our daughter and her husband as a gift. They promised to return it one day down the road. In 1988, they drove our first grandchild home from the hospital in that car and it was their daily driver from 1987-1991. After  that, they kept it well maintained and garaged until 2012.

By 1988, with kids raised, we were living in San Jose, California and I started to think about getting a first generation Camaro, my favorite muscle car. Driving down Story Road one day, I spotted a 1969 dark green metallic Camaro Sport Coupe with a "For Sale" sign. They were only asking $1800 and I knew I could swing it.

I've always been a fan of stock/original cars from the

1960s and I never wanted to own a hot rod or modified car. This one was a basic Camaro Sport Coupe, but pretty highly optioned. The decision was easy and I made it mine. Over the last 25 years, I've restored and repainted it back to better than original condition. It's a beautiful car that I am very proud of and for those years, it was my only "old" car.

In August 2012, I received a call from my daughter. She wanted to return the '67 Impala to us. It had been parked in their garage and covered for many years, but my son in law was into motorcycles and needed the space. For years, every time I visited I would look at that car and subtly hint that I wanted it back by saying "I want that car!" So, of course, I jumped at the chance to get her back and had her shipped from Sacramento, CA to Washington State, where I live now.

She refused to start when it was time to load her on the truck, and my son in law said, "She doesn't want to go!" She just needed to be pushed. When the delivery truck arrived at her new home, again she had to be pushed into the garage. I crawled under her and there were thousands of spider webs woven into all the parts, hanging off the tail pipe, and even hanging off the 12 bolt rear end. This car desperately needed some TLC.

The odometer read only 63,000 original miles, but the vinyl seat covers had gotten brittle with age and the cracks were covered with a towel. Getting it running was easy. I fixed some minor problems like loose wires and did a carburetor tune up, gave her some new fluids, and she was running great. Some of the gauges didn't work and one at a time, I was able to fix those small problems. She drove great then, but getting her to stop took some effort. She doesn't have power brakes, the four drum brakes were worn, and the master cylinder was shot. But, I fixed all of that myself.

The gas gauge did not work and I ended up installing a completely new gas tank and sending unit with the help  of some good friends, Cliff and Terry. The use of Terry's lift made it much easier to install. I ordered OEM seat covers and my car show buddy, Cliff, helped me install them over the course of a couple of days. We found some interesting things when removing the seats to work on the covers, including $1.79 in 1950-60s coins, hair ties, stickers from my grandchildren, and even hairpins from my mother-in-law. Transferring the original seat buttons from the old seat covers to the new ones was a little time consuming, but well worth it. I was hoping to find a build sheet under the back seat, but there was only a hand written paper with the VIN number and some factory option numbers. Of course, I saved that.

Under the hood, I cleaned up the original 327 V8 engine and very little touch up paint was needed. In 2013, I went to 20 car shows with the Impala and even won a few trophies. One great thing about this car is that it was my wife's Daddy's car and money is almost no object as far as she is concerned. So, when it needs something it gets it. The one exception to that rule would be the exterior paint. While fairly nice looking, even from a short distance, it's not perfect and that's just fine. She's been in the family since new and like all of us, this grand old lady has earned her few dings and minor scratches and I consider them badges of honor or marks of courage, if you will. She is a survivor and I think she likes her new home.

Budget Build Truck

By Gary M. Hughes

After years of being my trusty street rod navigator, parts washer, detail critic, and beer chaser, my wife thought it would be cool to have her own street rod. She was raised on a Nebraska farm and has been driving farm trucks since she was seven years old. Because of that, I was commissioned to build her a street rod farm truck. It was not to be fancy or extravagant, just something cute. We decided it would be a budget truck build and the quest for the perfect truck began.

For several months, I "shopped" by looking in barns or garages and decided the ideal truck would probably be a pre-war vehicle, say 1936 to 1940, though good ones are not easy to find. Just about that time, (2001) Mike DeTracy and his wife Janine both lost their lives in a tragic auto accident while they were on their way to  a car show. Mike was an avid car guy and I knew that he had just purchased a 1937 Chevrolet half ton pickup from a farm in Eastern Washington. I negotiated with Mike's brother to purchase the pickup and take over the project. It was not a creampuff by any means, but the budget build was underway.

With the body off of the frame and sitting in the corner, I was working on setting up the frame with Mustang suspension and "boxing" the frame rails to hold the weight of

the new V8 which is way too much motor for that little truck, even though there's no such thing as too much horsepower! My adult son came over to visit and suggested I put air suspension on the truck. I vetoed the idea almost immediately as there is no way I would consider such a major expense for a budget build.

That evening during a dinner conversation, my son brought up the air suspension again and my wife heard two words ... "cushy ride". The air suspension components arrived a couple weeks later. I kept saying to myself "nothing fancy or extravagant, just cute."

A couple months later, the frame was done and I was working on getting the cab ready. The same son suggested we convert the doors to suicide doors, shave the door handles, and set up remote access. Of, course I refused to consider that kind of expense for the budget build. That day

my son again went over my head and convinced the boss what needed to be done. Converting to suicide doors is a major task and my friend, Paul, and I spent many evenings creating the support for the hidden hinges and weight of the doors. Also the latches, hinges, and related components are really expensive. I kept saying to myself "nothing fancy or extravagant, just cute."

The bed was another story. With over sixty years of abuse and using the pickup for what it was designed for, the bed simply would not straighten. Buying the panels and possibly a tailgate to rebuild the bed was going to be a necessary expense. But hold on, son decides and convinces mom that we should have a "one off" custom bed designed and manufactured by Hank's Custom Beds. I really put my foot down that time and said there was no way I was going to that expense.

Two weeks later, I found myself sitting with Hank at his design table in Sacramento, CA. The bed has custom stake pockets, hidden hinges on a shaved tailgate with a "secret" opening mechanism, a frenched license plate, stainless bed strips, and flush mount tail lights to name a few of its features. It is a beauty and was delivered a few weeks later. I kept saying to myself "nothing fancy or extravagant, just cute"

Now, we had gone this far, so it only made sense to have some sort of exotic wood for the bed, dash, and running boards. Purple Heart, Teak, Bubinga, and several other varieties of exotic woods were considered. Finally, the choice was Appalachian Fiddle Back Maple. These boards had to be shipped from West Virginia, formed, planed, shaped, and finished to be perfect. I kept saying to myself "nothing fancy or extravagant, just cute".

While attending a car show, my wife saw paint colors she had to have for the truck. It had to be two-tone loaded with pearls, ice pearls, and special components to make it unique. This is the type of paint that provides Christmas bonuses to the employees of the auto paint and supply store. I kept saying to myself "nothing fancy or extravagant, just cute".

The upholstery had to be Ultra Leather with a custom design and even the underside of the dash has a custom  upholstered panel. I kept saying to myself "nothing fancy or extravagant, just cute".

Now that the project is completed, I should reevaluate my initial goals for the "Budget Build Truck" of "nothing fancy or extravagant, just cute" and see how I did. The dictionary defines "fancy" as "of superior grade; fine". Sorry honey, it turned out fancy. The dictionary defines "extravagant" as "exceeding reasonable bounds". Sorry honey, it is extravagant. The dictionary defines "budget" as "planned costs and expenses". Sorry honey, I failed there too. The dictionary defines "cute" as "delightfully pretty and precious". I NAILED THAT ONE!

One goal out of four on this project means she is twenty-five percent happy with me and my average is going up!

My Sweetie is a True 'Car Guy'

by Lloyd "Bud" Norton

In 1966, my wife Marilyn and I were living with our two year old daughter, Stephanie, in Sunnyvale, CA. We decided to replace our '59 Buick LeSabre two door hardtop with a new muscle car. Visiting auto dealerships along the El Camino Real, we looked at the Ford Fairlane GT, the Mercury Comet Cyclone GT, the Pontiac GTO, and finally the Olds 442. We fell in love with a White Olds Cutlass Holiday Coupe 442 with a black vinyl top and black interior and took it home.

A couple of months later, we loaded up the 442 and headed back to the Seattle, WA area to visit our families. The 442 was a great road car, very powerful, and comfortable. It was in Northern California in the foothills of the Siskiyou Mountains that a moment of revelation occurred. This portion of I-5 consisted, at the time, of two lanes and long sweeping turns with decent sight lines of up to a half a mile. It was in the late morning and there was little traffic. We were travelling at approximately 70 mph and passing slower vehicles as they presented themselves.

We came up behind an 18 wheeler and after a quick glance up ahead, I pulled out into the oncoming lane to pass the truck. But, something was terribly wrong. Coming at us at highway speed was a station wagon that I had missed. It appeared that he didn't see us, because he was not slowing down. We were in a terrible predicament, with a rocky mountainside on the left and the 18 wheeler on the right. There was no place to go and I slammed on the brakes so that I could dart back behind the truck. Unfortunately, the truck driver seeing our problem, also slammed on the brakes thinking that I would be able to pass and get in the right lane in time.

So, there we were slowing down side by side with the wagon still barreling down on us. My wife seeing what was happening, and while turning around in her seat to protect our daughter in the car seat in the back, yells out, "Oh my God, the car!" The truck driver finally realized what was happening and let up on the brakes. This provided the opening I needed to swing the 442 over just before the wagon whizzed by. He never did slow down and I doubt if he ever realized how close he came to being involved in a head on collision.

Now you might wonder why, with such a potential tragedy in the making, my wife would declare her fear for a mere hunk of mobile iron. Well, really, it was after all, a '66 Olds 442 and brand new to boot. So, it was obvious to me, and should be to all, that she is a true 'Car Guy'.

The Family Roadster

by Jeff Zurschmeide

"This story shall the good man teach his son; And Crispin Crispian shall ne'er go by, From this day to the ending of the world, But we in it shall be remember'd"
– William Shakespeare

For each of us in the car hobby, something happened to make us who we are. Something captured our imagination, or warped us forever, depending on how you look at it. For me, it was my father's purchase of a crusty old '59 MGA roadster in 1973. I was 9 years old at the time. I handed him wrenches and watched as he rebuilt the engine and worked on the brakes that summer. That was when I learned the difference between 7/16, 1/2, and 9/16.

The car was painted in British Racing Green when dad bought it. That seemed to me to be an appropriate color for the sweeping lines and snarling exhaust note of this car. The MG was so different from the boxy station wagons that populated our suburban neighborhood. It was a dashing, racy thing in a world of lumbering dinosaurs.

I recall how proud my dad was when a box arrived in the mail containing a brand new Nardi Classico steering wheel, and then when he threaded on a new walnut shift knob to replace MG's original plastic part. I also remember him carefully explaining to me the difference between a "convertible" and a "roadster." This was the beginning of an education that would lead to a career for me.

Dad raced the car in autocross competition with the San Diego Asebring Drivers throughout the early 1970s. The car made an infamous appearance in Fred Puhn's 1974 book "How To Make Your Car Handle" as an example of

what happens when you try hard cornering without a sway bar.

When I got to High School, my dad taught me to drive a stick shift in this car, running endless fig-ure-8s around the light poles at San Diego stadium, prac-ticing my second-to-third and back down. There was also learning the hand-brake technique for flawless starts on hills. He taught me how to properly drive a windy road through the hills. Driving became synonymous with wind in my hair and a sports car's response to throttle, gears, and steering.

Once in possession of my driver's license, I often used the groovy old MGA to take girls on dates. Pick a girl up in an MGA with the top down and take her to the beach for a sunset picnic and I guarantee she'll like that more than a burger and a movie. You may have heard it said, and it's true – MGA really does stand for "More Girl Action."

This story goes like many another. After I left for col-lege, the old roadster sat in the garage. Dad got older and chose larger and more comfortable cars, so no one was left to keep the old MG running. In 1995, Dad towed the car up to my home in Oregon and gave it to me. It was not drivable, and everything was sun-faded and generally tired. I pushed the venerable old roadster to the back of my workshop and swore I'd do it up right and impress my dad with it one day.

But, I lost my dad in 1997 and for a while it seemed as

if the MGA would sit as long in my garage as it had in his. Then in 2005, my wife suggested that we should restore it. She didn't have to say that twice. I decided on a total restoration and got the project started.

The biggest surprise of the project came when we looked at the VIN plate for a paint code. I'd noticed years before that the engine bay and trunk were a different color than the rest of the car, and it turns out this MGA was originally painted in a beautiful color called Glacier Blue, though any normal person would call it "Turquoise."

After six months of parts finding, bodywork and paint, and a few key upgrades like disc brakes and electronic ignition, the restoration was completed in May of 2006. Naturally, I had to show the car off. The MGA won a lot of trophies that summer, but the three that make me the most proud are first in class at the Portland Roadster Show, Honorable Mention at the Lake Oswego Heritage Car Show, and third in class at the All British Field Meet. Those shows stand out for me because of the large and excellent fields of cars they attract.

On the other hand, the car was never even in contention at the Forest Grove Concours D'Elegance. The old MG was docked points for the well-worn Nardi steering wheel and the aftermarket walnut shift knob, now burnished by decades of use under my father's hand and, of course, my own. If the judges entertained a thought that I'd remove either of those features, they were sorely mistaken.

In August of 2006, my wife and I entered the car in the Monte Shelton Northwest Classic Motor Rally and to our great delight we won the event overall! We've also taken the MGA on rallies with the Columbia Gorge MGA Club and Cascade Sports Car Club.

As a professional auto writer, driving this MGA is a singular experience. It simultaneously tells me how far the au-tomobile industry has come in the last 50-odd years and how wonderful a car can be with just the most basic features necessary to move people around. Driving the MGA is a pure experience of motoring. But more than that, this car has been with me since the beginning. It's part of me, and continues to generate fresh adventures every time the sun comes out (or not) and it's time to hit the road. This MGA is no trailer queen – it gets driven with the vigor its builders intended and as my father taught me.

I Can Do That

by Larry Montana

When I graduated from high school, I was working at the sawmill like many of the older guys that came and went before me. It was something that was available part time and fine while I was in school, but I wanted to get a job at a local auto body shop. Richter's Autobody got me into my first year apprenticeship and full time employment. It was like a dream come true.

I still was driving the '37 Chevrolet that I had painted with my Grandma's vacuum. It still had a very precarious steering box and front end and it drove like a fishing lure. The old farmer next door to me had helped me follow my dreams in building the car, including help in accomplishing some things that others had said, "You can't do that!"

With two weeks off in that summer of '76, before starting my apprenticeship, I found myself driving to the coast even though my car's steering was getting worse and felt like the front straight axle was going to fall out. My trusty ol' Chevy was on its last leg and I had no tools, no shop, and no money. I was about to become stranded when I found myself at Mission Raceway. There, I found someone to make a deal with and traded my '37 for a '66 Barracuda strip car that ran in the 10's. We clamped a couple of mufflers on it and I was homeward bound. The Barracuda was shelled out, meaning that everything had been removed to eliminate excess weight. Other than a driver's seat, there was absolutely no interior. With no noise dampening materials, it was definitely loud! The only thing it did besides shake and rattle was roll.

The brake rotors were so badly warped that the car could barely stop and with a spool posi rear end, it didn't turn very well either. The skinny pizza-cutter tires up front just compounded the maneuverability problem, but when you kicked in the six-pack on that powerful V8, it could only be called "Scary Fast." This car was designed just to go straight and I was returning home with that muscle to teach my hometown what fast really was!

I wasn't in town for more than 15 minutes before I was pulled over. After quite some time, and a lot of explaining on my part, the police allowed me to take the Barracuda home. The following months found me burning more than rubber. I was burning bridges with the locals and getting into too much trouble. I decided that I didn't need a different car, but I certainly needed a bigger town. So, without delay, I packed up, fired up, burned rubber out of town, and headed to the city of Kelowna B.C.

I walked into a normal looking shop, where I told them that I was a first year apprentice. Asked if I had any fiberglass experience, I told them about a canoe that I had made in school. That must have been good enough, because I was told to be in after lunch! And that was that.

When I walked thru the door of the Corvette shop, Boss Gill had pictures on the wall of him racing dragsters. There were Corvettes being cut up, custom kits getting glued on, and a Mustang with way too big of tires and wheels on it. I wanted to say what I'd been forced to listen for years… "You can't do that!" However, with my will to learn, I just shut up and learned. My head was swelled and swelling more. Suddenly, I was a Corvette customizer and hot rod builder. At only eighteen years old, I owned a fast car, had the girls, and some well-earned money! When I left Creston, one door had closed and one big one had opened.

The shop was sold to a Ford dealership in Fort McMurray, Alberta, but because I was known to be a hard worker, I was asked to help relocate the shop, and my life, to North Country. I quickly found myself saying, "Well, hell yah! Big money!" So, I entered the city of Ft. Mac, and standing in a big empty shop with a semi full of tools and another truck with a paint booth, I was told "Start building, Larry!"

So, I helped start the very first Ford dealership in Ft. Mac and was in charge of all operations. A short time before that, I wouldn't have even dreamed that possible. I had employees, two warranty jobs, and although I had not yet ever done a real paint job, I was running a Ford dealer's body shop. The world had opened up and it was a bit overwhelming to say the least.

After a few months, I was scheduled to be back for my apprenticeship course, my second year in Kelowna. It was all new cars and, despite my short time at the Ford store, I felt at a loss. Where were the racecars and customizing projects? I packed up in search of what I wanted to do, which was build cars! So, it was back to the people that knew what I wanted to know.

That is when I met Andy Stishanko, a customizer, back-yarder, and home-booth painter. With my knowledge of fiberglass, welding, and fabricating, I was hired. This is where I learned how to be a back-yarder, which 35 years later, I still am today. I have owned a few houses and built a few shops. I kept meeting more car builders and worked building cars for them. One of them was Keith Korecki. Keith is the owner of K&S Machine shop. We built plugs, molds, and other parts. And, we assembled racecars, one being a Pro Mod '67 Shelby. I also did many of his personal rides. The pace was hectic and I was living life in the fast lane.

I was always driving fast muscle cars and partying. I had the money and I had the drugs. I lived in a life of people telling me "YOU CAN'T DO THAT!" But, I did it anyway. Whether it was right or not, and I may have not taken the right road in life, I lived a wild, crazy, fast, and daredevil life.

I had never gone hang gliding. So, I did. I took lots of risks until I crashed. I raced on the street and got told, "You can't go that fast!" I did until I crashed and even ended up in jail. Believe me when the Government and the Police say, "You can't do that," they are right!

I moved away from the fast lane, back to my home-town, and regained my sanity. Still known as a car guy, I opened a shop and started building cars again. After the small town money guys had spent their cash, I decided to move again, intending to go back to Kelowna. Knowing there was lots of money there, but maybe trouble again, I stopped in a small town named Grand Forks and decided to stay. Over time, I built two shops and started down the fast lane once more. These days, I have pulled back a bit and downsized. I live the good life, doing what I enjoy and staying out of trouble. "I can do that!"

The Legend of Super Weasel Piss

by Steve Merryman

One afternoon, Tim and I were pulling the front clip on Tim's Suburban that had experienced a brief encounter with an elk a few days earlier.

"Hey, Tim. There are some nuts that are just so damn rusted I can't budge them and I'm afraid of snapping the heads off and I can't get the torch close enough in there to warm 'em up some. You got anything in your bag of tricks to bust them loose?"

"You ever tried Super Weasel Piss?"

With that simple question, the legend of Super Weasel Piss was born.

"Super Weasel Piss? You're joking, right?" Sometimes you never knew with Tim. This sounded just outlandish enough to be a real product, but then again one pant leg was going to need to be much longer than the other by the end of the day if my leg was being pulled. "OK, I'll bite. What is Super Weasel Piss?"

Tim walked over to the shelf on the side of his shop and started fumbling through stuff, his ever present cigarette dangling from his lips at an odd angle, a one inch ash hanging from the end. He suddenly threw me a small orange can. "Super Weasel Piss, great stuff."

I caught the 8-ounce spray can. It was nearly empty. I turned it so I could see the label that read Kano Kroil Penetrating Oil. "OK, I'll try it. Thanks. The can's about empty. Can I get it around here?"

"NAPA sells it sometimes, but they always seem to be out. If you find any, pick up a couple of cans for me, too."

The Super Weasel Piss worked pretty well. Nothing spectacular, but it worked as advertised. I didn't think much about Super Weasel Piss for a long time. I did find a couple of quart cans of the stuff and some spray cans. The spray is fine, but I like putting it in my oil can rather than spraying it.

I have a very good, longtime friend that I refer to as the Lil Red Haired Man. I love him like a brother, but that doesn't make him exempt from being the butt of a practical joke. The LRHM is not exactly the all-time leader in automotive repairs, but he will do his own maintenance on his MG-B and attempt an occasional repair.

One afternoon, he had his MG-B over and we were looking at the SU carburetors on the car. He wanted to take them off and was afraid he'd strip the threads if he reefed too hard.

"Bubba, over at the work bench, grab that blue oil can and squirt some of that on there. It should loosen them right up."

Five minutes later the carbs were off. It was apparent they needed some work.

"Hey, that's great stuff. What is it?"

"Super Weasel Piss." I tried to deadpan.

"Nah, what is it really?"

"Super Weasel Piss. I get it special down at the NAPA in town."

Now, you need to know that we had a good laugh over the name when I went and bought the cans originally. Chuck, at NAPA, has sold me a lot of things over the years and he thought it was pretty funny when I told him what Tim had called it.

We put the MG back together and the LRHM headed home. "I'm going to stop at NAPA and find out if you're BS'ing me about Weasel Piss. This sounds too phony to be true."

"Make sure it's Super Weasel Piss. Regular Weasel Piss doesn't work nearly as well."

As soon as he left, I ran into the house and called Chuck down at NAPA. "Chuck, remember the Super Weasel Piss story? Well I got a good friend headed your way."

A few weeks later, I stopped by the LRHM's house. He was out in the garage working on the car. I happened to notice a nearly new blue oil can sitting on the shelf.

"Yeah, they had one can sitting on the shelf behind the counter. Somebody brought it back and the guy gave me a real good deal. I can't find it anywhere though. Nothing on the Internet or anything. People just laugh."

It was all I could do to stifle the laugh. I probably ought to swing down to NAPA and settle up for the oil can and the can of Kroil.

Hoarding Corvairs

by Larry Carnes

My father was a collector. Well, kind of. In today's world, he would actually be called a hoarder. He was also high strung, compulsive, creative, generous, and many other things. Most of all, he was a great dad. He loved to buy and sell old cars and found out as a young father trying to make ends meet, that you could buy a car cheap and sell it for more money, and he really loved playing with the old cars. Sometimes he wouldn't sell them and so, the cars started multiplying around our house.

We lost my mother when I was 21, but she was around during most of the "car adventures" with my Dad. When she passed away suddenly and unexpectedly, he lost interest in cars and sold all of them, except for a brief foray into Lincoln Continental Mark III's. He remarried a year later after meeting a wonderful woman whom I believe my birth mother would have approved of.

We found out later in his life that he had been diagnosed with OCD … Obsessive Compulsive Disorder. And among all of the other things he could be called, he was a hoarder. He was not the type of hoarder you might see on TV these days with stacks of newspapers and garbage strewn around the house, however. He was fairly neat and organized. But, he was voracious in his collecting of things. A big part of his compulsion actually had nothing to do with "having" things. It was all about "the art of the deal." He loved to negotiate and when he sold something, it wasn't about profit, but simply making the deal.

One of the things Dad would obsess over was collecting tools and yard equipment. Who has 30 lawnmowers and piles of saws? Dad did. He also collected clocks. His obsessions didn't end there, however. He simply grew into larger things to collect... like his cars. He would spend hours at garage sales and possibly buy a car on the way to check out a list of garage sales or yard sales and possibly buy another car on the way home.

An obsession with Corvairs began one day when my sister's boyfriend pulled up to the house in one of them. It immediately caught Dad's eye and I guess he just couldn't shake the idea that he needed to have one or two or...

It started out with the understanding that I would need something to drive to school and by getting a car that we would work on together, it could be something for us to focus on and bring us closer to each other. It was a great idea and so, we went and found the first Corvair.

Then, he found another, and another, and another. His compulsion and obsessing grew into a collection so large that people often thought there was a Corvair convention going on in our driveway. More than once, strangers would come to the door and ask if this was the house where the party was being held. The answer was always the same. "No, those are just Dad's cars."

Since we lived in a suburban neighborhood, my father could not keep his entire collection of Corvairs at our house. So, he did what he could, which was to store his excess cars in my Grandparents respective barns on their farms. The farms were no longer active farms and there were several barns around with huge stalls, so this seemed like a good solution.

Obsessive with caring for the cars, as well, he purchased heavy car tarps designed for the Corvairs and would cover them while they sat. Other preparations included insuring the gas tanks were full and had a "gas stabilizer" solution he had purchased and putting mice traps in the cars to take care of any rodents that might invade them. Not a perfect solution, but the best option we had.

Once a month the family would make a trip to visit the Grandparents. We would first arrive at my mother's parents' house and after my dad exchanged pleasantries, it

was time for him and me to get to work. We would go to each car carrying the proper sized battery and fire them off one at a time.

I would then back one out and we would check all the tires and fluids, and then ease the car out of the driveway. I would go down the road at a leisurely pace until the engine was warmed up and then take my hands off the wheel and slam on the brakes to see if the wheel jerked, suggesting a stuck brake drum or other issue. Then, I'd back up and slam on the brakes again for good measure.

Upon completing those visual and physical tests, I would pull over to a quiet spot in a nearby church parking lot and just listen to the motor. It was so quiet in the country that I could easily hear any strange sounds coming from the engine that warranted attention. I would also get out and look under the car for strange leaks such as brake fluid, oil, or transmission fluid and check the oil level one more time. Having completed those checks, I would get into the car and buckle up for the real fun. I would turn the car down a curvy road and proceed to drive at a decent clip, attacking each turn as if I was in a rally race, accelerating at high speed (or as much as the 6 cylinder air cooled engine could give) and shift as fast as I could. Since the Corvair had four wheel independent suspension, this was actually quite fun!

I would then head back for the next car and repeat the process until all of the cars were done at my first set of Grandparents and we would then proceed to the next set of cars about 30 minutes down the road at my father's mother's house (my Dad's father had passed on years earlier).

One day, we were finishing up a set of cars at my dad's family home and were at the last car when my dad suddenly opened the passenger door and said "I want to go with you!" This surprised me, as he generally preferred to hang around the barn, but I was glad for a chance to share his company, so I pulled out. I went through my normal routine (except for the 'rally racing') and as we were getting close to my grandmother's driveway, I gave the little car some more gas and my father immediately said "Slow down!" I replied "I've got it, no worries!" and pushed in the clutch with my left foot, pressed the brake pedal with my right foot, and the brake pedal shot to the floor! No Brakes!

I immediately slammed the car into third gear while popping the clutch and yanking the wheel to the right and gave the car more gas. We slid into the gravel driveway sideways while my dad yelled something unintelligible. I quickly turned the wheel to the left while slamming the car into second gear to straighten it out and we slid up to the front of the barn as I yanked up the emergency brake handle under the dash on the left side and turned the car off.

I was proud that I had not wrecked the car. Richard Petty would have been proud! As I began basking in the glory of Richard Petty's praise going through my mind, I turned to my dad who yelled "GIVE ME YOUR LICENSE!!" I stammered "But Dad, the brakes were out!"

He reached over and pressed the brake with his foot and the brake pedal held! I slid out of the driver's seat  and handed him the license from my wallet. He snatched it away from me and placed it in his shirt pocket while sliding himself into the driver's seat. He looked at me and yelled "You'll never drive any of my cars again!" through the window. He cranked the car up and popped the clutch, pulling the car into the barn and then ... drove the car straight through the rear barn wall.

He turned the car off and stepped out of it while looking at the front end protruding through the back end of the barn (It wasn't damaged TOO badly). I stood in the driveway doing my best to stifle my giggles, blood tricking down my chin as I bit my lip. He walked back and stood beside me, handing me back my license and said quietly "The brakes don't work, we might want to look at that" and walked off to his mother's house.

I don't obsess about cars, but still really enjoy them. Funny thing ... every time I see a Corvair, I think of my Dad!

Remembering Toro

by Mark Heller

I have always had a passion for cars. My parents were not car people and didn't even own one until 1970 when I was six years old. It was a '67 Beetle. This was an epic fail for a kid who had a grandfather that worked at the Chrysler plant in Newark, Delaware and drove a '68 Fury and another grandfather that had a '68 Coronet. Dad later redeemed himself by buying a '71 Galaxie 500.

My first weekend car fling was the previous year in 1969 when dad rented a sky blue four door '70 Cutlass for a weekend road trip. We had a great time right up to the point of having to take the car back to the rental agency. I still have the vision of it driving away and me crying on the bus trip home.

My mom was an artist and I spent much of my free time drawing car pictures under her tutelage. When my grandfather was ill, I would make cards with car drawings for him. I sent them to him right up to the day he passed in 1972. This was a sad moment, but my car drawings and a ride in my Uncle Johnny's new Olds Omega helped to lift my spirits. Earlier that year my dad brought home a Consumer Reports Car Guide and one car in particular caught my eye. It was the '72 Gran Torino with the coke bottle shape and oblong octagonal headlights. It was the coolest car I had ever seen in my entire eight years. This was the four door. You can imagine how excited I was when I saw my first fastback on the road and the inspiration it provided to my drawings for years to come.

By December 1983, I was 19 and living in Northern Virginia. My best friend, Kenny, had a '68 Chevy II with a 396 V8 that we cruised around during our high school time. He would borrow his stepfather's cool '74 Charger SE when the Nova wasn't running for one reason or other. I had drained my savings with my first car, a '75 VW Rabbit, and was looking for a car that would fit within a $500 budget. Many deals fell through, including a '76 Nova, an AMC Hornet and a '72 Country Squire with no reverse.

One day, about a week before Christmas, I looked at the classifieds (back in the days before Craigslist) and saw an  ad for a '72 Torino. I called the owner, Manuel. He said his son now had a Mustang and no longer wanted it. Kenny drove me to Manuel's house in Oakton, which was about 15 minutes from where I lived.

Expecting just a regular Torino, I followed him around back and there sat a '72 Gran Torino Sport fastback! Originally maroon and repainted white (very poorly with no prep), it was now sporting mid '70s LTD hubcaps. The quarters had an ample amount of rust and the driver's side looked like someone had sanded it with a cheese grater, but I didn't care. I turned the key and the 351 Cleveland roared and tapped to me as the gauges glowed. I put the loose column shifter into drive and drove it round the block. It needed 4 new tires, a front end rebuild, and exhaust, but I knew I could not pass this opportunity up. Manuel was asking $700 and I offered $500. He told me to get the cash and we had a deal.

Even though it had an expired inspection sticker, I took my chances and drove it to work. At this point, I had had enough of riding the bus. I worked in the warehouse of Best Products and some of my younger coworkers laughed at me when I pulled in, but unlike them at least I didn't need mommy and daddy to buy my car for me. Nicknames like "Gran Torusto" were bestowed on me, but this car was like a bull so, I decided the nickname "Toro" was an appropriate moniker.

Things with Toro were going great until one day when we had a sleet storm and I slid straight into a Volvo 240. Toro's grill was smashed and nose piece dented, but otherwise we were both ok. On the way home, I landed in a ditch and had to be towed out the next morning. Other than a bunch of dirt, Toro survived that, as well. Shaken, but not stirred, I drove Toro to Pennsylvania which was a 3 hour drive. The heater did not work and there was a hole in the driver's floorboard, both of which made the trip quite interesting.

In January I hit another ice patch and took out the back of a VW Dasher. At this point, I knew I needed to take Toro off the road until I could make the needed repairs. Since I was making minimum wage, it took a few months before I could save up enough money for the repairs needed to pass inspection. Once in a while, if there was no snow I would drive Toro at night around the neighborhood, cranking the Audiovox cassette deck way up. During the day, taking the bus to work became torture.

Finally, in April, I was back on the road and overtime was offered during a renovation at work. So, I of course did what every mature 19 year old would do … weekend trips to the beach! Toro made multiple trips to Virginia Beach. I had a friend that was from there, so we had a free place to stay each time. On one of the trips going through the

Hampton Tunnel, I floored it while blasting an Iron Maiden tape and hit close to 100MPH. It is a memory I will never forget.

In the summer, with the help of Kenny and cheap beer, I started on the bodywork. Neither of us lived in a house with a space to work on cars, so we went to the basketball court near my apartment and started the sanding. The white paint job had not been prepped properly when it was done, so it chipped off rather easily. Surprisingly, the spray can red-oxide primer came out fairly well. I found some baby moons and trim rings at the local Trak Auto and painted the rims black. I even found a body shop that would finish it and paint it for $700. Many colors were considered but the plan was to paint Toro red and keep the trim black. Finally, Toro would no longer be laughed at, but admired by all.

Unfortunately, I was never able to complete the vision. Fall arrived and there was no more overtime and Toro's exhaust decided it was a good time to fall off, taking the manifold bolts with it. I used the money I was saving for the paint job to get headers and a new exhaust. The lifter tap got louder, the floorboard hole got bigger, and the column shifter was to the point you could barely get it into drive. I was facing the reality that Toro's days as a daily driver were numbered.

About a week before Thanksgiving, I was working in the warehouse when one of my co-workers, Tracy, pulled up to the loading dock in a '74 cherry red Mustang II. The body was perfect, other than a few minor scratches, and the white vinyl top was flawless. Its black interior looked like it came right off the showroom. I told her how nice the car looked and she told me she was considering selling it and getting something new. Of course, I asked how much and she said she was trying to get $650 for it. I told her I was interested and would let her know, if it was still available after Thanksgiving.

I drove up to Pennsylvania with Toro knowing this may be the last time we made this journey together. Ironically, this is the best he had run in a few months. I knew the decision I had to make was not going to be an easy one, but the Mustang II was too good to pass up. I only had $400 in the bank, so with my paycheck I was going to offer Tracy $500 and hope for the best.

When I came into work Friday, I saw Tracy at the morning staff meeting. Before I could make my offer she came up to me and informed me that the Mustang II was not starting right and she was getting a new car over the weekend. If I came up with $200, she said it was mine. I went to the bank after work was over and the deal was done!

I got it started and while driving home I realized what a great buy I had been blessed with. The four banger was a little tired and the muffler was coming off, but other than that the Mustang II ran like a new car. I bought a new muffler, paid a guy at Midas $5 to install it, and it purred like a kitten. The starting issue turned out to be a defective casting in the carb that was blocking the choke spring. I filed it down and it started the first time!

Of course, euphoria turned into reality when I looked at Toro in the driveway. Since I was renting a room from my friend's mother, there was no way I could keep both cars. I needed to find a home for Toro. I remembered my friend, Steve, was looking for a car and sold him Toro for $200. Steve paid me $100 down and would pay me $50 biweekly for the other half. Interest came in the form of sharing a six pack of the cheapest beer available.

When Steve made the first payment, he brought Toro with him and we went for a ride with a six pack in tow. I was very happy with the Mustang II, but still wondered if there might have been a way to keep both cars. About 20 minutes into the ride, Steve let me drive. Once I got behind the wheel, I knew the decision was going to haunt me for years to come. Watching them drive away, I had this sick feeling in my stomach that I had done the wrong thing.

In Late February of 1985, I was on my way to a friend's house and made a left turn that I had made a hundred times before. Unfortunately I was not paying attention to the median barrier they had recently built and catapulted the Mustang II into the air, landing on the other side of the road, head on into a '78 Monte Carlo turning the other way. In shock and my knee bloodied, but ok otherwise, I laid on the ground and looked at the wrecked vehicles. The Monte Carlo was driven by one of my co-workers at Best who recognized me first. Both cars were destroyed. I was soon surprised by a cab who was backing up to help, nearly running over me with his tire.

The next morning Kenny, his Uncle Dave, and I went to the tow yard to look at the damage. The Mustang II was a total loss. I stood back about 20 feet from it, hoping that since it was red it could imitate Christine and restore itself, but no luck. Where is Arnie Cunningham when you need him?

On the ride home, Kenny told me that Steve had parked Toro. He had neglected the brakes and seized the calipers. In addition, he had attempted to silence the lifter tap with 50 Weight oil in the dead of winter. Regardless of the devastation, I saw this as an opportunity to get Toro back. I called him up and offered him $400, which was all I had. He declined, saying his father was planning to help him get it running.

Disappointed, I moved on and bought a '71 Corona. It was a reliable, but boring ride. So, when Kenny offered to let me take over payments on his '74 Monte Carlo, I jumped at the chance. It was a beautiful brown and tan with a 350 V8 and swivel buckets. Kenny had added Cherry Bomb mufflers and a Mitsubishi stereo to make it even sweeter.

I got a call from Steve in June of 1985 saying that Toro had been towed from his neighborhood and I could have it if I paid the tow fee. I had my hands full keeping up the expenses of the Monte Carlo, so I am not sure what motivated me to jump at the chance. What Steve forgot to tell me is he left the title in the glove box. When we got to the tow yard, there was Toro with the oblong oval headlights, sadly looking at me. We went to the counter and the lady told me that I needed the owner's permission to get the title. I suspected they had ulterior motives. Several phone attempts to contact the owner proved fruitless. With its accumulating storage fees and bills of my own, I had to give up the fight.

Thirty years have passed and along with that a marriage, two stepsons, and three grandkids. Currently, I live in Florida and I am in the process of restoring my '81 Camaro which was my stepson's first car. Every now and then I have a recurring dream that I have found Toro in a barn in rural Maryland where it had been sitting for the last 30 years.

I walk up to the windshield and confirm the serial number, as I do every time I see one. At this point in my life, I don't know what I would do if I really did find it. But still, I wonder ... what if that day at the tow yard had gone differently?

Still In the Game

by Denny Hall

This isn't a story of triumphant street-racing or impressive car builds, but about a teenager trying to get on the road with some modicum of style. I started lobbying for a car that I could "work on" when I was fifteen. I man-

aged to convince the parents that it would be good for me, so we started looking.

The first one got away, and it truly was a car of the "one that got away" category: a one-owner '41 Ford coupe that had been traded in at the local Ford dealer. The salesman my dad normally dealt with called him when it came in. Unfortunately, the day he found out about it was a day that I was so extremely

car struck that I found it impossible to attend school. A couple of delinquent friends, and my delinquent self, spent the day roaming around town. I vividly remember lying on a stranger's lawn that day, gazing at the two yellow coupes on the front cover of the September 1959 issue of Rod and

Custom magazine that I had been carrying around in my back pocket.

As fate would have it, I picked the wrong time to let the car affliction rule me. The school sunk to the lowest depths of their charter and chose that day to question my absence by calling my home. Busted!

The '41 coupe went on to a possibly more deserving, but certainly less loving person. It was probably some old guy who would drive it until the wheels fell off and never even think to "dago" it or provide an inexpensive set of baldies for the wheels.

About six months before my 16th birthday, I managed to renegotiate my needs with my parents and the hunt was on once again.

My girlfriend's brother-in-law knew someone who had a '47 Ford club coupe for sale for $125. It was a little beat up, but it ran well. So, I bought it.

Because this was still about six months before my birthday, I couldn't take it out on the road. Couldn't? Aww, that's not the American way. The Northern Pacific depot, where my dad worked before they shut it down, had an eighth-mile dirt-and-gravel road behind it that was private property. It was about a block from home, so I was able to drive the car up and down that road to practice speed shifting. I'm really surprised that the transmission lasted until I got my license.

On more than a couple of occasions, I failed to stop and turn around where the road met 6th Ave. and ended up in the town of Steilacoom, which could be reached by back roads in those days. The trips were more fun when they were forbidden.

I had a friend with me on one of those trips, and on the return home we ran out of gas in University Place. The gauge didn't work, but I was sure there was plenty in the tank. It happens.

We just kept coasting, knowing it was all downhill to where the car should be. There was only one traffic light and two stop signs on the route. We made the green light in the most congested area and kept on coasting, and then ran the stop sign at 19th Street and another one at 6th Ave., allowing us to roll into the parking lot at the depot. Across the street was a grocery store/gas station where we bought a few cents' worth of gas and when my dad came home from work, he drove the car the block and a half to our house.

Looking ahead to the all-important birthday, I put the car in our one-car garage and started to fool with it. I smoothed a small dent in the top with Bondo and filled the hood. My dad worked for the Northern Pacific Railway and ran the depot at the South Tacoma shops. The machinists and welders at the shop could make anything you wanted and since my dad handed out the paychecks, they were always very accommodating.

I gave him the front shackles and he had the boys make some longer ones. That gave it a rake. Now, here is where we see the difference between today and the '50s and early '60s. I had a deck lid that needed considerable work and two rear fenders that were also whacked. Fixable, but why bother. I bought good replacements from a friend for about $15. No bodywork needed. Bolted them on. Done.

I had a solid, smooth, rust-free body, which I wet sanded until my hands bled. The next step was going to cost about the same as the price of the car. I worked at my grandfather's shingle mill for a few days and was paid way more than I was worth because my grandmother wrote out the checks. This enabled me to have C&F Body Shop fill the trunk lid and paint the coupe Ford Torch Red. I bought the baldies I needed and some scavenger pipes. I couldn't afford white walls for the front, but I had plans.

The car came home on my birthday. That was a Friday and my dad couldn't take me to the driver's test until the next day, which gave me time to mask and paint the dash with spray cans of Torch Red. The next morning I passed the test, and as soon as I got home, I tore off the masking paper and hit the road.

That '47 Ford coupe, a '55 Ford two door, a '54 Merc hardtop, and a '46 Ford convertible took me through high school. I didn't have them all at once, of course, but I got one after the other and I was never without a cool car.

In 1960, I joined the Stompers car club and was with them a couple of years. The Stompers wanted to raise some money to finish their Chrysler powered Fiat Topolino so we decided to have a dance at the Crescent Ballroom and hired the Wailers, which were not only one of our favorite local bands, but a nationwide success, as well. We did a great job and met our goal of raising what we thought was a substantial amount of money. The president of the Stompers was so impressed with the idea that he quit the club to become a promoter. The Fiat was never finished.

When the Stompers faded, I joined the Drag-ons. Nobody in the Drag-ons had a car that was show ready at that moment except my '46 Ford convertible. It was a nice car and the old original paint polished up well. I had the interior done in white rolls and pleats and with it being lowered and sporting my buddy Dick Page's wheels and baldy hub caps (baby moons), it represented the club in fine form at the Push Rods Motorama in Hoquiam. There was no competition in the semi custom convertible class and they had the trophy ... so, I got it!

I'm a musician and artist by nature, still recording and playing whenever I can. During my early years after high school, the people playing traditional American and Euro folk music, which I got into, were of a different mindset than the teenage hot rodder. Our focus was on art, music, literature and politics. Mine still is but I've made room for hot rods. At the time though, it was more in character for me to drive a sports car. I had some pretty cool sports cars, including a '59 Bug Eyed Sprite, a '57 Jaguar XK140 that seemed to drive like a truck after the Sprite, a brand new '64 Sprite, and finally, a '53 Porsche coupe.

The demands of travel and needing a vehicle to haul luggage and instruments led me to the other end of the automotive spectrum. Yes, I started buying vans. They did the job comfortably and I bought and sold several of them.

I got back into old cars by fate. It was always a festering interest ... an itch in the back of my mind that wasn't getting scratched. One day, when I picked up a copy of Street Rodder magazine, it hit me like a ton of bricks. I was missing the hot rods and decided I needed to follow my own interests. Now to some, my combination of interests was eccentric, but I've always been comfortable with that. It just put more fun in my life.

So, I'm still in the game and my stable of cars now include a full custom '41 Ford coupe built by Donn Lowe, a '28 Ford roadster PU, and I'm working on Dick Page's old '32 Ford roadster that I acquired a while back.

The Stompers car club is still around, too ... unofficially. There are no meetings, officers, or much going on, but that's the way we like it. Today, three of us old boys from the Stompers have old cars and we tracked down and had the same company do up replicas of the original Stompers jackets. One day, an old girlfriend asked me, "Do you want your old car club plaque back?" Well, of course I did and once I had it, we decided to get them re-popped for the other guys.

I've come to the conclusion that old cars are a very good thing for me. They keep me young at heart and I enjoy the people who share this interest. There is a lot of good will among these people.

Lucky

by Mike VerValin

Iwas lucky enough to ride with my dad on a special produce delivery up near Mt. Rainer early one Saturday morning. Riding high up in the big truck cab, there was a view of everything all around me. For a ten year old, it seemed like flying. The best part was that we had left the city behind and were venturing into uncharted lands. Well, at least they were for me. It was easy back then to see where the city ended and the open country began. As we headed out of Tacoma, Pacific Avenue became referred to as "the Mountain Highway".

Along the route, we passed a cool looking lot with all kinds of cars, trucks, and machinery. I asked my dad about the place. He said it belonged to a guy named "Lucky" and he was a bit of a horse trader, though horses weren't necessarily involved. That's where he had bought the new box for the big truck.

Dad had seen this nice 16ft. enclosed truck box sitting on blocks and inquired about it. Lucky said it wasn't particularly for sale as that's where he kept his welding supplies. The way dad told it was that before the conversation was over, a deal was struck and Lucky agreed to sell, including new paint and installation on dad's '56 Ford 2 ton truck. It seems there were two horse traders that day.

I made a mental note of its location and didn't think it was that far from home and I could tell that there was much more to see than a handful of cars and trucks here. It was a treasure land of other cool old stuff that my young eyes had focused briefly on as we sailed past it on the Mountain Highway. Lucky's place needed much further investigation.

I told my friend at school about the place and the next Saturday, loaded with peanut butter and jelly sandwiches stuffed in my army surplus bag and his army canteen filled with Tang roped to his handle bars, we set off by bicycle to find Lucky's place. We had carefully planned this on the Q.T. and left extremely early, because we were going out into the unknown and didn't know how long it would take to return. We quietly met on my corner at 7:00 AM, when we thought no one would be up.

By mid-morning, it was already getting warm out and it seemed to take forever to find our destination. Maybe it was farther than I thought, but we eventually saw it up ahead. As we rolled onto the lot, all was quiet. There was not a car, truck, person, or even a stray dog in sight up and down the four lanes of the mountain highway. Perfect for poking around really cool old stuff. As our tires crunched the gravel, we dismounted and walked our bikes from there and quietly leaned them against the building.

My friend and I read and collected old car books from the 1920's and 1930's, even some earlier and also had a cool collection of radiator caps, hub caps, tail light lenses, starting cranks, headlight buckets, and anything else we deemed old and particularly cool. We were really into it and had found tons of this stuff in berry bushes and piles of "junk" on all of the old farms outside of town. A really good source was a shed that had collapsed flat to the ground after many years. It was always good for something rusty. We looked at all of this old stuff as if each piece was a jewel and Lucky's place was a new found gold mine and a young collector's dream.

We started looking at the front line of cars, talking

about grills and bumpers and looking for 'twin exhaust', a sure indication of power. But, looking at the nicer cars up in front was quick and halfhearted. What caught our eyes were the really old fixer uppers in the back against the fence. In a few years, they would be affordable if I saved my berry picking money and if Aunt Millie was still good for her 'Cash in a Card' at Christmas. But, the creme de la creme, as it turned out, was the cement block building we had leaned our bikes against. It reminded me of an old gas station and it had several huge glass windows. However, these windows had been covered over by a wild assortment of boards, parts of signs, and almost anything else that was available to obscure them from prying eyes. This just screamed "Go away and don't look." So what's a kid gonna do?

We peered through the space between boards and the dirty glass with little success, though there was the occasional glimpse of alluring shapes with polished metal frames and glass to fuel the fire. My buddy noticed that the boards didn't go all the way to the top of the windows. We needed to get higher. All around the building were things like oil drums, pallets, tires and rims, boxes, and such. With great care, we piled one atop the other… just high enough to peer into the building. It worked!

With hands cupped to the glass and literally out of our minds with excitement, we were describing to each other what we were seeing, though neither of us were hardly paying attention to what the other was saying. While hanging on to boards and balancing on stacked trash, there came a voice from right behind us! "Would you like to see inside?"

If I hadn't already sweated out the crap I had drank from my friend's canteen, I surely would have pissed myself. Both of our heads spun around and our jaws dropped like a sack of concrete. My "partner in crime" fell from his perch and bounced three times before coming to rest between his bike and a very greasy old oil drum. I couldn't move if my life depended on it due to the white knuckle grip I had on the top board covering the window.

I've heard that a drowning man can have his whole life flash before him in the blink of an eye. I'm here to say this phenomenon occurs to a smaller extent in an event such as this. In the blink of an eye, I thought number one, we're dead, either by this guy or my folks; number two, if I'm allowed to live, this summer is toast; number three, I thought we were the only ones on the planet awake at this time of the morning; and four, he asked us if we wanted to see inside?

As the blood returned to my head and my face regained color, I realized he didn't yell at us. I still think of that to this day. In a clear and gracious tone, it was as if he asked "Would you like cheese on that burger today, sir?" Almost on cue we both said "Uh ... Yeah ... Sure ... "

As we jumped down onto solid ground and began dusting ourselves off, he was singling out a key on a large ring and said his name was Lucky. We in turn told him ours. Though he seemed nice enough, I was a bit leery. This guy was thin and fit with really black hair slicked back, wearing a very white T-shirt and Levi's with the cuffs turned up over black boots. I sized him up. I'd seen this kind of guy in the movies. He was definitely a motorcycle guy or maybe a rebel of some kind. But, throwing caution to the wind, so to speak, I had to risk all and see what kind of cars were in here.

He opened the little wooden side door and we all three stepped inside. No lights were turned on, but slowly our eyes became acclimated. The rays of the sun shot through the narrow spaces between makeshift slats on the windows and dust floated through them giving it all a very mystical look. It was if we had stepped back in time.

It's still vivid in my memory. It most certainly was dark and everything was black, the cars silhouetted in the minimal light of the square cave. The cars were huge open Touring cars and Phaetons that when compared to my ten year old size were extremely tall. I climbed aboard and got behind the wheel of a Touring car with diamond tuck leather seats. There were cars with jump seats, side mounts, and clincher wheels. A President of the U.S.A. had ridden in one of the cars. Some wore wooden wheels. The impressive array of cars were mostly from the twenties, maybe one teen, and another mid-thirties. I do remember what I believe was a Pierce Arrow, with its unmistakable fender mounted headlights and red accents. We all three looked and talked about the cars. My buddy and I mostly listened. We looked at castings, cut glass, leather straps, lenses, and more. The floor space was crowded and I remember a

raised level in the back with all sorts of auto related service and advertising signs, called memorabilia these days.

As my friend and I were checking out an unusual wheel and tire, Lucky said "Close the door when you leave". I looked up in time to see his striking silhouette outlined by the bright sun as he walked out the side door. That was the first and last time I saw him, but certainly not the last time I heard about him.

We gave one last glance around at the cars that seemed to be peacefully sleeping under the dust. The sun was blinding as we closed the door behind us. This had been a spiritual experience for us two young enthusiasts and I don't think my friend and I said more than a dozen words to each other all the way home.

When we closed the door to Lucky's building that day, a much bigger door was opened and has remained so to this day. I continued to learn about cars and their history, collecting some along the way. Lucky's building still stands and still bears the Lucky's Sales sign.

Harold "Lucky" LeMay continued collecting cars and memorabilia and making history, as well. When he passed at age 81 in November of 2000, he had amassed one of the world's largest car collections. A portion of his collection went to the state of the art facility in Tacoma, WA, known as LeMay – America's Car Museum. The majority of the collection was retained by the LeMay Family Collection Foundation on the historic grounds of Marymount Military Academy.

I will never forget my brief and inspiring meeting with Lucky! Thanks Mr. LeMay!

In Memory

I Wanted to Join the Prowlers

by Bob Biehler

Editor's Note: As part of my hunt for stories from old car guys across the country, I put out the word on Facebook, a popular social media site on the internet. I simply ask people to email their stories to me. One day, I found the story below posted directly to my Facebook page. The story was too short and the accompanying photo was very blurry. But, it was a great story! I immediately wrote back to him and asked him to call me. Well, he did and we talked for about 45 minutes.

Bob Biehler was a very interesting character and he had stories and pictures that he was eager to share for the book. He thought it was a great idea and wanted to be a part of it. So, we made arrangements to meet the next week at his shop. That meeting never happened.

Sadly, Bob passed away suddenly and unexpectedly the next morning. I met with his wife, Tanya, a few weeks later and we developed several stories about Bob which appear in the first book and in this book. But, this story is directly from Bob, the original story that he posted on my Facebook page and the beginning of some wonderful relationships I have developed with his family and friends since his passing.

My name is Bob Biehler. I'm an old hot rod guy from San Diego. Just a few months from hitting 70, I'm still in the game and havin' fun! When I was in school, we cruised the burger joints and the best place in town was Oscars, because you could get a Coke for a dime from a car hop on skates and wait for the Prowlers to cruise through.

The Prowlers is one of the oldest clubs in the country, started in 1947. These guys still have the "bitchinest" cars. My biggest goal in life was to someday have a car cool

enough to join the Prowlers.

I had a few pretty rough hot rods, but when I got out of the Air Force, I started building a full fendered '23 Model T roadster. It turned out pretty cool and we were cruzin'. Every year, the Prowlers have a picnic and we were invited. We cruised in and parked right in the middle of all the coolest cars in town. WOW! We were havin' fun now.

Well old Bob, being a beer drinker at the time, started right in. After a while, they had a chug-a-lug contest so, of course, I had to get involved in that. Shortly after, I was hammered and planked out on a picnic table when a member of the Prowlers, Bruce Hamilton, came up to me and asked me if I would be interested in joining their club. The only word I could get out without puking was "Noooo!"

Well that ended my dream. Don't let alcohol get in the way of your dreams!

The Paul Hansen Touch

by Tim Strange

Many people come into our lives and change us ... some for the better and some for the worse. Some change your life so much, that they also touch the lives of many around you. This is the case with my friend, Paul Hansen.

We met Paul and Erik Hansen at the Detroit Autorama the year they had their Moal built/Hollenbeck sprayed '32 Ford in the running for the Ridler Award. I found them to be awesome, energetic people from the start. They made the Great Eight that weekend, but did not win the Ridler. Later that winter, we met once again at Blackie's Invitational Fresno Car Show where we had our purple '54 Chevy on display. They won the big award for the rods that weekend. Later on, they won the America's Most Beautiful Roadster title with their '32. I was not there, but remember reading about them winning and was happy for their grabbing one of the most respected awards in hot rodding.

Fast forward a little ... We had a cool '52 Buick custom project that we were doing in our shop with only one full time employee. That project was for what was probably the worse client we've ever had. He was hiding it from his wife and when she found out, a ton of crap was thrown our way. I could write a whole book of stories from just this aspect of the project. The Buick sat unfinished for almost two years, during which time we had to let our one employee go.

We had put the unfinished custom project up for sale on a couple of online sites. Well, if you have every tried to sell an unfinished project, it's very tough to do, especially with cuts started and tack welds holding the shape. It is quite simply, very hard for most people to see the vision of the finished project. We'd had a few phone calls on the

project, but no one really understood the plan and design for this car until the phone rang on one very special day. It was Paul Hansen calling.

He asked if I remembered him and his son Erik. Of course, I did. We talked for a while about the AMBR and other things in life since we had last seen each other. Then, the conversation shifted to the Buick project. I talked about my ideas and he talked about Erik and him wanting to build a custom as a father and son project. It was very cool that they understood the vision and could see the project in their heads like real car guys do. I was hopeful, but I had doubts about whether their project would be the Buick, sitting, waiting for just the right guy to come along. After all, this wasn't the first time the phone had rang and I had explained the dream to someone.

They surprised me and said they wanted the project, but they didn't want to just buy it and haul it away. They wanted us to do the project together! I got off the call and sat there in disbelief, excited all the same.

Plans were made to meet up at the next Grand National Roadster Show in California. We were also including an artist and automotive designer, Brian Stupskis', from Problem Child Kustoms to help put things on paper and give an artist's input on ideas and style.

Excitement was building as we met at the little air field down from the show for breakfast. Plans and ideas were thrown around about building a real quality custom. For some that don't know, most of the west coast built customs are pretty on the outside, but can leave a little to be desired both under the hood and underside of a car. We planned not to hold back in any area on the car and decided a great name for her would be "Resilience". Through the build, there were numerous calls and fly-in meetings, all while making great memories and better friendships.

Paul (and Erik) Hansen came to the shop at a time when we most needed him. Through the crap from that stalled '52 Buick project, we were very close to closing up shop and leaving the world of hot rodding ... forever.

Some of my best buddies came to help and thrash for the next year or so. Along the way, that shop time together with my buddies, Shawn, Dave, and Chuck, along with my very supportive wife Carrie, generated memories and funny stories that none of us will ever forget. One of those friends was going through a real rough time at home and this time in the shop with this buddies was exactly what he needed. This project revival was not only a saving grace for us at the shop, but had started having the same affect with others.

Through the building of this project, we spent money at different suppliers around the country. From parts suppliers, engine guys, and machines shops, this car helped their businesses, put food on their tables, and helped make some payroll ... in part, thanks to Paul Hansen. It also helped us with our BMX race team, the cash flow allowing us to help get some of the kids better equipment and positive times at the track. Thanks to, in part, Paul Hansen.

Once finished, we toured this custom Buick from Pomona to Sacramento to Tulsa to Detroit to Fresno; all of the major indoor shows. I had displayed at some, but not all of those west coast events, and it was always a dream to have my work on display at major shows. The Hansen '52 Buick project helped me achieve that dream.

The graciousness and class of Paul Hansen was also evident to us during the weekend of the first outing in  Pomona. He took all of us that had invested so much of ourselves into the project out to a very nice dinner with his family. He gave a moving speech that touched all of us. I also tried to give a speech. I wanted to thank him for the chance and his trust to build this project. But, I was getting choked up, tears filling my eyes, as I recounted how Paul came into our lives at a time when we most needed it for the shop.

Yes, we won some decent awards at some of the major events, including Best Custom to Celebrity Pics to Fine Nine awards. However, it is the memories of setting up, cleaning the car, and the dinners with Paul and Erik that stick in my head as the important memories. As we started show-ing outdoors, the big win for the summer was the KKOA Leadsled Spectacular Award in Salina Kansas, where we received the 777 award. This is the top of the custom awards. A permanent trophy is on display in the National Rod and Custom Hall of Fame museum in Oklahoma that includes the names of the winning owners and builders … cool stuff.

In fact, the Hansen '52 Buick went on to be featured in many magazines around the world, including covers and national ad campaigns.

This assignment was also one of the first big projects that Brian Stupskis', from Problem Child Kustom, was a part of. Brian has since gone on to be a part of teams that have won just about everything in hot rodding ... maybe due to a little help from Paul Hansen, also.

Where is this car now? Through Paul Hansen's generosity, it is now part of the collection at the Peterson Auto Museum in Los Angeles. I get goose bumps just thinking of that. Thanks again to Paul Hansen.

Paul (and Erik) was my "one Client". Paul was that one client that fully believed in the shared vision of a project and in my team and me. He allowed to us turn that vision into a reality for him. But, he was more than that, having been a travel partner, dinner companion, and friend.

How does "one client" change your world? Well, this is where people that don't do this for a living are starting to get a little lost in the story, but it is where the value of Paul Hansen shows up in the lives of many people. For that year or so of building the project, it put food on the table and clothing on Carrie and me. It helped a buddy through a rough time and it gave all of us buddies lifelong stories and bonding time. And the story and Paul's impact on me didn't end there.

I had the Buick on display at SEMA that year. At the end of the day, I was wiping off all the day's dust and fingerprints when Kevin Tetz came up and introduced himself. Kevin was the host of the Trucks TV show and invited me to come and volunteer on an episode of his show. WOW, that was cool. So, I did go to Nashville during the next year to help on the TV show which evolved into me hosting the Search & Restore TV show for two full seasons. Again, thanks to in some part, Paul Hansen.

As a result of doing that show, which worked by getting my buddies and volunteers to come and help, we built cars for eight great individuals. Most of those individuals and their families say we really changed their lives for the positive in a time when they most needed something good to come their way. Again, in part, thanks to Paul Hansen.

All of those volunteers that came to help got a lot of personal exposure and many of them have had their businesses grow because of that show, putting food on their tables and adding more employees, helping those people out also. Some have even gone on to do other TV shows. Again, thanks in part, to Paul Hansen.

All of this came from one chance meeting at a car show, a phone call, and in the end, Paul's ability to see the vision

of an awesome project.

There are untold amounts of father and son stories of Paul and Eric being a part of the build and, as a result, all of the travel and bonding from that experience will stay with Erik forever. Too many parents just don't do this enough, but that's the kind of guy Paul Hansen was.

From that one call, he literally changed hundreds of people's lives in very positive ways. Aside from his very successful career, Paul Hansen's involvement in the hot rod community made lots of things possible for many people that might not have happened had it not been for his passing through their lives.

So, thank you Paul Hansen for coming to us in a time when we most needed someone like you. We, and the many others you touched, are better people because of you and will be forever in your debt. Thanks for everything, buddy.

RIP my friend!

Commando Power

by Mike Godwin

Editor's Note: Mike Godwin submitted this story to me in February 2014. He had been a huge supporter of the first book in The Old Car Nut Book series and was looking forward to being included in book two. Sadly, Mike passed away on May 8, 2014. He will be missed, but here is a part of him that will be with us always.

By some off chance, should you ever find yourself in Tacoma, Washington around the middle of December, locate Sixth Ave. and drop into the Golden Sail diner. Now, this is not a foodie tip, as they do not serve any real noteworthy food at this location. Like a diner that can be found in any number of other locations, they are just serving up good home-style grub and breakfast is available all day long.

As you enter, you'll notice a set of booths to the right and to the left is the typical long counter service area with a row of tables further to the left. In the back is a small room that is used for private parties or meetings. This room is of interest because for the past 30 years a small group of aging gentlemen has gathered here to relive their youth.

The stories rarely change and the outcome of any race is always the same with the storyteller winning the race hands down. In their youth, Sixth Ave was the street to cruise and stop light racing was their passion. So, these folks tend to forget how fast the cars really were and the

251

speeds do seem a little unrealistic to the person hearing the story for the first time.

For those up on the local Social Scene, you'll note a retired Appeals Court Judge, a State Representative, a couple of businessmen and one of the best ambulance chaser lawyers the area has ever seen. Actually, they all look like what they are; middle to late sixties guys that get together to hash out old stories and have breakfast.

The December 2013 gathering had a twist in the form of a surprise guest by the name of Lois. A surprise, as this gathering had always been an all-male enclave. Seems a couple of people had invited Lois just to make sure that yours truly got a good dose of Humble Pie early in the day.

After exchanging social greetings and a few warm hugs, Lois settled into a chair nearly directly across the table from me. It did not take long for the question about Commando Power to surface at the table. You see, Lois had been known to slam a few gears in her little Jeep and she'd had no problem holding her own.

One evening many years ago, as a bunch of us sat in the parking lot of a burger place, she arrived in a '64 Sport Fury. It was a nice looking car for the most part, but it was a boat all the same. We started talking about the car and Lois indicated that it was pretty quick. I looked at the front fender and spotted the emblem that declared it was equipped with a V8 engine. Smiling, I figured a whopping 318 two barrel resided under the hood. So, my alligator mouth began to overload my humming bird backside once again.

It wasn't long and the two of us were exchanging verbal snips while the rest of the crowd just watched. It probably would have ended there until Lois declared that the Plymouth had something called Commando Power under the hood. Of course, with a lightweight Ranchero packing a '66 289 V8 with a four barrel, there was no reason for me to worry about Commando Power. Her "sled" even had full size wheel covers that held some dorky looking three spoke attachment. "Put it on the street" was my battle cry, which drew a round of cheer from the guys.

To her credit, Lois did not miss a beat. She simply reached into her pocket, pulled out her keys, and headed for the Plymouth. We lined up at the first light, headed toward the Tacoma Narrows Bridge. I slipped the Ranchero into low and started a little Power Brake action. I was planning my entire victory run as I waited for the light to turn green. Not too much gas at launch, let the RPM climb, then get second, and hammer the four barrel.

The light went to green and I smiled as Lois had failed to Power brake that heavy old Plymouth at all. About mid intersection, I grabbed second and just as I was going to slam the go button to the floor, I heard it just off to my left. WHOOSH . . . the huge white whale went past me. The next three lights were repeats of the first, as Lois took me to the woodshed, stop light after stop light.

We were at the final light and she gave a hand signal that she would run the bridge against me. Sort of a "If your man enough" type challenge. Not a problem, as I just knew that this time I would take her on that long run out over the Tacoma Narrows Bridge. The light turned green. I gave the light in the rear Ranchero a little more gas than I should have, and it fishtailed a time or two. Then, once under control, I dropped the hammer again. By now, the taillights of the white Plymouth were moving away quickly. I pressed on, but soon, the clacking of valves gave me cause to look at the gauges that were mounted under the dash. The water temperature was headed into the danger zone and the oil pressure was dropping like a rock. It was time to back off and just run at the posted speed limit.

On the other side of the bridge, I pulled into the weigh station as was customary with racers to review the race. Lois was kind enough to open the hood on her white sled and show me what a Commando Power motor was. Her dad, a tinkerer from way back, had put a 361 cubic inch Cross Ram engine with two four barrels into the sleeper Fury. It was no wonder Lois had such confidence. Being the lady she was, she offered me the chance to try again on the return trip back to Tacoma, but I declined that opportunity.

So, here I sat with several of my buds and Lois some 46 years later reliving one of the worst street racing beatings that I had ever received. Thanks a lot gang. Can we choose someone else for next year?

Rocks and Squirrels

by David Dickinson as told by Tanya Biehler and Aaron Hall
in memory of Bob Biehler 1942-2012

Many people knew Bob Biehler as a hot rod builder and Bonneville Land Speed motorcycle racer, but he was much more than that. He did much more than build cars, race his bike, and go to car shows.

Bob was not only physical in applying his mechanical skills. He was also a skilled diver and, for a time, applied that talent in his work en-vironment. This wasn't because he was hired as a diver, but because he hap-pened to be able to and being on scene made a dif-ference in the project and to  Bob. He also loved diving for abalone with friends and did that as often as he could. He purchased a 41 foot commer-cial fishing boat from one of his diving friends, repaired the non-running straight 8 marine engine and took it fish-ing with his family and friends.

The boat was named the PJ and was a documented vessel. This meant that Bob had to take an oath and sign special papers. This made Bob a Captain. He loved that he was Captain Bob. He was even legally able to perform mar-riages if he was three miles out to sea. While it was an adventure to own such a boat and fun was had on it many times, mooring it was as expensive as our mortgage on the house. So, it eventually sailed away to a new owner.

An old art form that is not practiced much anymore is that of Water Witching or dousing, as it is sometimes called.

Some people are adamant that water witching provides results in searching for water. Others think it is hog wash. There was never a discussion in Bob's mind. He knew it worked and was proficient in this rare talent, as well. He was a bit unconventional in his water witching, however. Bob didn't use a tree branch. Nope, he used two metal coat hangers and got great results, both in California and the Pacific Northwest.

One time in Alpine, California, he and Tanya bought a 3.47 acre property. The land had very shallow granite bedrock. Most wells had to be dug to a depth of 300 to 1400 feet to find consistent water. Bob found water at twenty-eight

feet and the well was dug an additional one-hundred feet to ensure a steady flow. The water always flowed and there was never a problem with the shallow and affordable well.

Hunting was a past time that Bob enjoyed for many years, not only for the hunting, but for the hiking, as well. He loved being out in the woods and just being in nature. Like most things in life, Bob wanted the hunting to be interesting, so he would hunt with a black powder rifle or a bow. On one trip to

Quilcene, he got a deer and a bear. Both skins are at the family home still.

If he wasn't on the trail of an animal, he may be looking at the ground, hoping to spot a "bitchen" rock. He loved rocks and was always picking them up and admiring them. Some he would keep and some he would leave for someone else to find. He had no intention of polishing or displaying them. He gave them away.

Many a kid got a rock. Bob would give them to his son and daughter and then to grandkids when they came along. "Here's a special rock just for you", he might say or "Put this in your pocket for good luck!" There were always more cool rocks to find and Bob knew how to find them. Lots of times those young ones would bring rocks to Bob and he'd accept each one as if it was the most unique and beautiful rock ever seen, much less held by human hands. He made the kids feel good.

The driveway leading to the house is lined with rocks, rocks, and more rocks. It was a minor passion, but one he gave time to quite often. In his Southern California days, Bob not only went rock hunting, he was on the lookout for rattlesnakes, as well. The stick he created with a special loop and pull string for rattlesnakes sits in the corner of the living room where his unique forms of art dominate.

One time while looking for rocks, he discovered an area where it was obvious that native Indians had lived. The artifacts included broken bits of pottery and a large arrow head that would have been used on a spear. Tanya's research revealed that it was shaped like those found dating back ten-thousand years. To this day that arrow head is amazingly sharp to the touch and would be as effective as it was when it was first shaped by its maker. It was one of Bob's treasures and he had many.

Bob's hunting days ended in 1991 when Tanya was diagnosed with breast cancer. He was distraught. How would he endure if something happened to his lovely bride? Bob told God if He would spare Tanya and not take her away from him, he would never kill a living thing again for as long as he lived. He was good to his word in spades. If he saw a worm in the gravel driveway, he would pick it up and set it in the garden.

Bob's shop was surrounded by trees, so you can imagine the critters he had around there. He often worked with the doors open and little brown squirrels would forage around near the shop. Bob decided to start feeding one who would come up to the door and watch him work. So, he began putting nuts in the front pocket of his hooded sweatshirt as a stash. He would lure the squirrel in and eventually had it eating out of his hand.

After a few weeks of feeding this pet squirrel, the little dude figured out where Bob was keeping his stash of nuts and started running up his pant leg, into his front hoodie pouch and getting his own nut. He would go up one leg, into the pouch, out the other side and down Bob's other leg. Bob was getting a kick out of his little pet until he realized there was more than one squirrel.

One day, two squirrels showed up; one running up each leg and meeting in the middle inside his shirt pocket. You can imagine Bob's surprise when they started fighting over the nuts in his shirt! He stood there unable to do anything until they finally shot out from his pocket and scurried out the big door of the shop. He stopped feeding them after that.

Bob and Tanya decided that having the squirrels run around the shop was not a good idea and they had become a safety issue. You can't have wild animals running through your pockets when you're cutting or welding or crawling under part of a car. Then there was the issue of grandkids and the possibility of them getting bitten. The squirrels would need to be moved in the gentlest way possible and taken a reasonable distance away, so they wouldn't come right back. By the time it was over, Bob had trapped and released eight squirrels. He must have thought to himself, "No wonder that little guy kept showing up so much!"

Bob devised a trap and caught each one as it came for its daily entitlement. He and Tanya found a place a mile or so away that they felt would be a good spot and sent them on their way. He missed the squirrels once they were gone. They had been his little buddies.

Bob Biehler was a man's man with a big soft spot in his heart. He cared about everything and everyone.

About David Dickinson
Creator and Editor

The Old Car Nut Book

As a child, I would lay around the living room, playing with my Lincoln logs, designing homes and landscape designs that would include lots of parking spaces for all of the cars I planned to own. As a teenager, I bought my first '56 Chevrolet BelAir with the money I had saved from working on farms, in restaurants, delivering newspapers ... anything that would pay me so I could get a car when I turned 16. From then on, it was all about keeping the car running to its peak performance and cruising around showing the world my great little ride!

Like everyone else, I had to grow up. Well, kind of. I guess I never got away from cars. As the years roll by, like the odometer on an old car, I keep checking off the miles ... and the cars in my past. I always seem to be looking for my next pride and joy. I've had countless cars and there are stories for every one of them. I still change cars often, but wish I could keep every one of them.

I started out by writing my own stories, a few of which appeared in book one. More of them are included in this second book in The Old Car Nut Book series, but I have more stories to share and so do the rest of the old car nuts in America. The Old Car Nut Book is my way of sharing the dream with other Old Car Nuts. It is also my way of reaching out to younger car nuts beginning their journeys and fulfilling their dreams. I think it's important to know where the pioneers of the car enthusiast world came from.

As these first two books gain popularity, stories will continue to be gathered and more editions put into print. The response from current contributors, potential contributors and others, anxious to read these stories, has been tremendous.

I plan to compile at least four volumes of *The Old Car Nut Book*. Book Three will be all about "Road Trips" and Book Four will be all about "Racing". You can be in one of these upcoming books by sending your story in now.

Have a great story, but concerned that you don't write well enough? That's OK. Send it in and let me do what I do. Together, we'll collaborate and turn your story into one you can be proud to share! Go to www.OldCarNutBook.com and click "How To Submit" in the menu for details. You can also contact me directly at Contact@OldCarNutBook. com or 206-497-3197.

I hope you have enjoyed this book and look forward to seeing your nose buried in another volume of The Old Car Nut Book. In the meantime ... tell others, please!

Made in the USA
Monee, IL
10 December 2023

48766768R00157